What people are saying about …

OVERRATED

"It can be fashionable to talk about the poor but not as fashionable to talk to the poor. It may be popular to talk about justice and still not know any victims of injustice. But we will never make poverty history until we make poverty personal. Eugene Cho shatters all our hipster coffee-shop talk of justice and dares you to dive into the trenches and do something real with your life."

Shane Claiborne, author, activist, and friend of Eugene Cho

"A gutsy and gritty exposé on the motives of a generation in love with the idea of saving the world, *Overrated* by Eugene Cho is a necessary exercise for all who desire to truly be a part of the change God wants to bring to humanity. This book is real, personal, necessary, and a must-read, so we can all continue on the path toward justice for all."

Louie Giglio, Passion City Church/ Passion Conferences

"When you're done talking about the gospel and are ready for your walking to be the gospel: Start here. I needed this book."

Ann Voskamp, author of the *New York Times* bestseller *One Thousand Gifts*

"I am so grateful for Eugene Cho and his passion to show Jesus's love to a needy world in tangible, practical ways. His message is relevant and challenging. This book will inspire you to help establish authentic justice in society today."

Judah Smith, lead pastor of the City Church, Seattle, and *New York Times* bestselling author of *Jesus Is _____*.

"In *Overrated*, Eugene Cho offers an honest and necessary confession on behalf of the church. Through powerful and enlightening stories, Eugene Cho offers a timely reminder of the cost of discipleship in the pursuit of God's work of justice."

Soong-Chan Rah, Milton B. Engebretson associate professor of church growth and evangelism at North Park Theological Seminary and author of *The Next Evangelicalism*

"How incredible would it be if everyone took this message to heart, that the body of Christ would be the first people the world turned to for solutions to society's problems? I stand alongside Eugene in challenging all followers of Christ to embrace the calling on their lives, serve their communities, and step into the untold potential of a life spent serving others."

Pastor Matthew Barnett, senior pastor of Angelus Temple and cofounder of the Dream Center

"Eugene's questions became mine: I love justice, but do I actually live justly? Am I committed and disciplined enough to become an expert about causes and issues I care about? Is my activism smart?

Is it grounded in prayerfulness? Do I incarnate the gospel in such a way that I compel people toward Christ? *Overrated* challenged and chastised me, inspired and energized me. I highly recommend it."

Lynne Hybels, cofounder of Willow
Creek Community Church and author
of *Nice Girls Don't Change the World*

"Eugene Cho asks—and answers—a question that everyone who seeks to live out their faith in public at some point asks: Am I more interested in the idea of changing the world than actually doing it? *Overrated* wrestles with this question with Eugene's signature humor and grace. I recommend it for anyone who wants to authentically live their faith in public—to actually do what we say we believe in."

Jim Wallis, *New York Times* bestselling author
of *On God's Side*, president of Sojourners,
and editor-in-chief of *Sojourners* magazine

"True justice begins in our own hearts. It is small and personal before it is world changing. We need to take Pastor Cho's message to heart."

Rich Stearns, president of World Vision U.S. and
author of *Unfinished* and *The Hole in Our Gospel*

"Through a vulnerable and humorous lens, Eugene shares his personal story of how God revealed to him His own heart for justice and that as a disciple of Christ, there is always a cost. So go and change the world … but bring this book in tow."

Jenny Yang, vice president of advocacy
and policy at World Relief

"*Overrated* is a gospel gut check; Eugene's personal story will have readers examining their work on behalf of the kingdom in a new way, and leaves us more honest, effective, and ultimately better disciples of Christ."

Joshua DuBois, bestselling author
of *The President's Devotional*

"This deeply personal narrative takes readers on a lived journey of wrestling through the realities of being a justice fighter today. I encourage all believers to read *Overrated*. It lays a course for how we must proceed as humble but faithful justice leaders in an unjust world."

Dr. John M. Perkins, cofounder of Christian
Community Development Association
and author of *Let Justice Roll Down*

"Eugene Cho's words paint such a beautiful picture of what justice is, and could be, that your heart races with anticipation to join God in spreading His justice across the canvas of planet earth. *Overrated* is a marvelous book."

Derwin L. Gray, lead pastor of Transformation
Church and author of *Limitless Life*

"Calling all world changers, change agents, justice seekers, and leaders: this book is for you. This is Eugene's story, his confession, and I'm better for reading this book—and you will be too. I'm inspired, challenged, provoked, and equipped to live a life more in line with my calling and ultimate pursuit of Jesus."

Brad Lomenick, author of *The Catalyst Leader*

"Eugene Cho calls to light our obsession with glamorous ideals of world changing that we have disassociated from personal, real-life investment and sacrifice. This honest approach encourages us to pray, discern, and listen to God's prompting that His grace would not only be the foundation of change in us but of our desire to change the world."

Ken Wytsma, president of Kilns College, founder of the Justice Conference, and author of *Pursuing Justice*

"Get ready for an extremely honest and self-revealing journey that has the potential to radically change your life as it prepares you to radically change the world. Eugene Cho encourages us to move beyond the hype of just telling a good story toward living a life that is ultimately for the other—the life that Christ invites all of us into!"

Rev. Dr. Brenda Salter McNeil, assistant professor of reconciliation studies at Seattle Pacific University

"Finally, someone has written a book that will burst everyone's feel-good justice bubble! With disarming honesty and a heap of hard-earned, practical wisdom, Cho powerfully argues that the pursuit of self-sacrificial justice is at the heart of following Christ and invites readers to truly participate in Christ's stirring resurrection by first sharing in His nitty-gritty death."

Christena Cleveland, PhD, author of *Disunity in Christ*

"Eugene Cho reminds us of the gift and challenge of costly discipleship. *Overrated* is a must-read for anyone who pursues justice out of a deep commitment to Jesus. With his unique and transparent confession, Eugene invites us to cruciform justice work that bears the fruit of personal transformation. What a gift!"

Revs. Gabriel and Jeanette Salguero, colead pastors of the Lamb's Church and cofounders of the National Latino Evangelical Coalition

"Part confession, part challenge, *Overrated* is a long-needed conversation about how we do justly, love mercy, and walk humbly with our God. Too often, we confuse hashtags and selfies with the work of justice because we love the idea of changing the world. This book is both practical and theological, inspiring and sobering, empowering and educating."

Sarah Bessey, author of *Jesus Feminist*

"There are very few people I meet who are willing to live out their convictions with the sincerity, humility, commitment, and sacrifice that Eugene Cho has shown. This book challenges us all to bring dignity forth through our storytelling and remember that the work we do is not about us, and never has been."

Scott Harrison, founder and CEO of charity: water

"There's a subtle, toxic deception that any of us can fall into as we seek to 'make a difference' in this world—before we've even realized the lie, we've made the work about ourselves. This book will challenge you at every level of your daily life, yet without presenting a crushing load; it will deepen your desire to know God, to pray and talk with Him, and deeply connect with others on the journey."

Bethany H. Hoang, director of the IJM Institute for Biblical Justice

EUGENE CHO

OVERRATED

ARE WE MORE IN LOVE WITH THE IDEA OF CHANGING
THE WORLD THAN ACTUALLY CHANGING THE WORLD?

David C Cook®
transforming lives together

OVERRATED
Published by David C Cook
4050 Lee Vance View
Colorado Springs, CO 80918 U.S.A.

David C Cook Distribution Canada
55 Woodslee Avenue, Paris, Ontario, Canada N3L 3E5

David C Cook U.K., Kingsway Communications
Eastbourne, East Sussex BN23 6NT, England

The graphic circle C logo is a registered trademark of David C Cook.

The website addresses recommended throughout this book are offered as a
resource to you. These websites are not intended in any way to be or imply an
endorsement on the part of David C Cook, nor do we vouch for their content.

Unless otherwise noted, all Scripture quotations are taken from the Holy Bible,
New International Version®, NIV®. Copyright © 1973, 2011 by Biblica, Inc.™ Used
by permission of Zondervan. All rights reserved worldwide. www.zondervan.com.

LCCN 2014940384
ISBN 978-0-7814-1112-7
eISBN 978-0-7814-1236-0

© 2014 Eugene Cho

The Team: Alex Field, Nick Lee, Helen Macdonald, Amy Konyndyk, Karen Athen
Cover Design: Justin Pae

Printed in the United States of America
First Edition 2014

1 2 3 4 5 6 7 8 9 10

062314

CONTENTS

ACKNOWLEDGMENTS

I am nothing apart from the gospel. Thank You, Jesus, for Your mercy and grace.

No person is an island to themselves. People have invested in me, encouraged me, prayed for me, and believed in me. As such, this book is dedicated to all of you.

To my wife, Minhee: Without you, this book would not have been possible. You are in each and every chapter. Thank you for your love and friendship. Thank you for your prayers, patience, and courage. In you, I see, witness, and experience the substance and sufficiency of God's grace. I love you.

To my children, Jubilee, Trinity, and Jedi: You all bring me such joy. I am so blessed and proud to be your father. Thank you for your grace, especially during the many nights I locked myself in my office to finish this book. While I am filled with anticipation of how God will use all of you for His glory, I am constantly reminded that God is using you now.

To my parents: You are my heroes. To this day, I don't quite know how you did it. You sacrificed so much for your three sons. Thank you for your courage and devotion. Thank you for not only loving the idea of a better life for your children but fiercely and prayerfully pursuing it.

To Quest Church: You are my family. Minhee and I are so grateful to have planted this church. Thank you for allowing us to play a role in your lives, for doing life together, for your commitment to the kingdom, and for enduring my very long sermons. Thank you for entertaining my NBA dreams. Special thanks to the handful of folks who helped start the church: Jin, George, Leah, Joanie, Becky, Dan and Megan, and Gordon and Stacy, and others.

To the church and café staff: Ray, Gail, Joanie, Katey, Pam, Jin An, Matt, Roxy, Christian, Jill, Sun, Aaron, Coby, Brenda, Liz, Carrie, Josh, Jake, Randall, and Chewy. Gratitude to all the elders (Barbara, Tim, and Jin Kim), deacons, and community group leaders of the church. It's a true honor to serve alongside each of you. #OneTeam

To the team at One Day's Wages: Cindy and Jason, Michael and Stephanie, Jason and Jinny, Steve and Mary Jane, Philip, Julia, Melissa, and all of our interns, volunteer staff, and advisory board (Carla, Jack, and Trace). To the thousands around the world who have partnered with us. It's true: We don't have to be rock stars, celebrities, or millionaires to make an impact in the world.

Last but not least, thanks to those who helped make this book possible. Special gratitude to Derek Sciba who helped me organize my words; Chris Park, my agent, who helped me to realize that it was time; Justin Roboto Pae who helped design the book cover; Alex Field, my editor; Helen Macdonald, ruthless and master wordsmith copyeditor; and the entire team at David C Cook.

To God be all glory and honor.

FOREWORD

I'm grateful for people like Eugene Cho who take the time to think about justice and then try to do something about it. This book is an introduction to justice for those who are curious about what it means, what the buzz is about, and how they can get involved. In a way, Eugene is trying to understand it himself. And he's doing something more—he's trying to understand his own selfishness and the tendency to play the role of hero by using the poor. It's a very real problem, and Eugene is a very rare person to admit it.

This kind of personality crisis, I think, is experienced by most of us. We get involved in an issue because, these days, you can become a rock star by wearing the right clothes and caring about the poor. You'll get no judgment from me. I remember those days myself. But once we're through that phase, what can we actually do? Do we really have the power to move the needle in the lives of the oppressed?

What was even more meaningful about this book is that Eugene turned the spotlight toward the heart of God. As a pastor, he reminds us how much God cares about justice, how much His heart wants to right the wrongs in the world, and how much He wants us to be involved in that work. The issue of justice can easily be over-spiritualized and turn quickly into theological conversations rather than practical action, which is one of the reasons even religious folk often turn to secular pursuits of justice. They just want to get something done and stop talking about it. And so I appreciated Eugene's blending of the thinking about it with the doing something about it.

The question I asked after putting the book down was simple, though: What can I do? What practical thing can I do to move the needle in the lives of people who have been treated unjustly? My wife and I have a company and provide jobs, which is perhaps the most fulfilling experience of my life. To us, that's moving the needle on justice. But this book made us want to explore more and do more. We are, then, like many who will read this book: busy, curious, hopeful, and distracted. And this book was a welcome call to focus and reflect and, of course, act.

Justice is a complicated issue, but Eugene reminds us the solution doesn't have to be as complicated as the issue itself. We can do something. We can contribute.

Donald Miller
Author of Blue Like Jazz *and* To Own a Dragon

INTRODUCTION

This book is my personal confession—honest and sometimes painful, because in these pages I share pieces from the story of my broken life.

I admit to being more in love with the *idea* of changing the world ... *than actually changing the world.*

And in wanting to change the world, I confess to neglecting a posture of humility in which I must be aware that *I, too, must change.*

I don't think I am alone in this neglect.

I've shared this confession with many people—individually and in larger groups—and I've received my share of pushback. But surprisingly, I've also received a fair amount of support from people who have resonated with the crux of this book. In other words, they felt they understood this sentiment and even admitted to the same offense. I've received thousands of letters about how this challenging message has profoundly spoken to them, and how, in various ways, it has encouraged them to more deeply and courageously live out their faith in Christ.

My greatest hope for this book is that it will encourage those who want to change the world: the activists, leaders, justice seekers, doers, humanitarians, and philanthropists in all of us. My hope is also to encourage the broader church, both locally and globally, especially in its pursuit of seeking justice and pursuing the dreams and visions that God has deposited in the hearts of those who love Him.

Ideas, dreams, and visions don't change the world. Rather, it's people—like you and me, who faithfully, prayerfully, and tenaciously live out these ideas, dreams, and visions—who change the world.

I love Christ, and I love the church.

I love people, and I love the privilege of encouraging and exhorting them.

I especially love young people and feel truly blessed to speak, mentor, and invest in this and coming generations.

I love reminding, calling, and prompting all people to the purposes of God.

My hope and prayer behind this book is to call people to a deeper engagement to the purposes of God, to "act justly and to love mercy and to walk humbly with [their] God" (Mic. 6:8).

We live in a world and culture in which—both out of privilege and conviction—many people want to make an impact. This is good. In fact, this is *really* good. This desire needs to be affirmed, nurtured, and cultivated.

However, let's be honest with ourselves. We all love justice and compassion. Seriously, who doesn't? But is it possible we are more in love with the *idea* of compassion and justice than we are with actually putting it into practice?

Is it possible that we all love compassion and justice ... *until there's a personal cost* to living compassionately, loving mercy, and seeking justice?

I hope that being overrated is simply my own confession. However, if in some way it is also yours, I'm grateful for the gift of grace and courage that allows us to examine ourselves, enabling us to grow deeper, wiser, and more emboldened to live in a manner that reflects God's hope, beauty, and love.

It's my hope we can examine how we engage our calling to follow Christ, and examine how we love mercy, seek justice, and walk humbly with God. Because it's not just about us doing justice; this journey is also about allowing the work of justice to change us. In other words, we not only seek justice as we follow Jesus, but we seek to *live justly*. Our calling is not simply to change the world, but perhaps as important, our calling is to be changed ourselves.

This book is about my journey in learning this truth. It's a book that describes a very personal collision of faith, justice, following Jesus, praxis, and counting the costs. It's messy and painful, but it's real. And it's my invitation to others to be less infatuated with telling a good story and instead be more determined to simply live a good story—a story of faith, hope, courage, sacrifice, and justice. It's a call for deeper discipleship.

Yes, this book is my confession.

My aim isn't to motivate anyone using shame, guilt, or fear. While some may use those tactics to motivate, they are simply not sustainable. And to be blunt, they do not honor God.

The chapters that follow are an attempt to encourage you to "count the costs" of following Jesus, because the endeavors of loving mercy, seeking justice, and walking humbly are not isolated pursuits but rather an integral part of the journey we call discipleship.

Overrated? Perhaps.

But all I know is that if you're reading this paragraph right now, you're still breathing and alive. And together, we have an opportunity to courageously examine ourselves through the mirror of God's grace.

God isn't done with you yet.

God isn't done with me yet.

God isn't done with us.

Chapter 1

COUCH SURFING: OUR STORY

Family meetings are common in the Cho household. I playfully have to remind the kids who their daddy is.

However, I knew one particular family meeting on a summer evening in 2009 would be difficult and emotional. There would not be a lot of joking around. I had more lowlights to share than highlights. Actually, I had *only* lowlights to share. (Maybe the heat wave had something to do with it. Yes, it actually does happen in Seattle. When temperatures hit the nineties, the entire city freaks out. Some even stop recycling when a heat wave strikes. Trust me—that's serious for my city.)

The events that led up to this family meeting transpired quickly. It was almost as if my wife, Minhee, and I were just coming to terms with the news ourselves as we announced it to our children.

Minhee and I ushered our three children into our bedroom that Wednesday evening. The kids knew Mom and Dad had been under

some stress—despite our best efforts to play it cool and composed—
and I could tell they were apprehensive.

I didn't quite know how to articulate it, so I told them, plain
and simple:

> Kids … first, we want you to know that Mom and
> Dad love you all very much. So very much. As you
> know, our family made a commitment, to God and
> to people, to donate one year of our wages to help
> people who are extremely poor around the world,
> by starting a new organization called One Day's
> Wages. Unfortunately, we're struggling a bit and
> have fallen short of our goal. We need to come up
> with some money. So, we really need your under-
> standing. We need to leave our home for about
> ten weeks. We need to clean the house because …
> we're leaving in two days. Everyone gets to take one
> bag, so go to your rooms tonight and start packing.
> We're not sure exactly where we'll be staying, but
> we'll figure it out.

Our eldest daughter, Jubilee, just eleven years old at the time,
burst into tears. She was convinced we were going bankrupt (even
though she was clueless to the meaning of the word). She bluntly
asked, "Are we becoming homeless?"

Our middle child, Trinity, age nine, was very anxious and ner-
vous about the idea. Not knowing exactly what all this meant, tears
welled in her eyes.

Our seven-year-old son, Jedi, on the other hand, thought it might be fun because he could only equate this to a very long sleepover. He simply asked if we could take our Nintendo Wii console. God bless Jedi. (The force is strong with this little one.)

As for Minhee ... you could say that she was not pleased.

Yes, you can say that.

Just the day before, I listed our family home as a short-term rental without conferring with my wife. Yes, that was not a typo.

I was both bored and desperate, and in that perfect convergence of boredom, desperation, "what if" thinking, and crazy faith, I crafted an ad on Craigslist to sublet our home for $10,000—thinking, *Who would pay $10,000 for two months?*

Did I mention that I did this without first consulting my wife, because seriously, *Who would pay that much?*

(Note: Don't put an ad on Craigslist to sublet your home without first consulting your spouse. And if you do, do not mention my name or this book.)

And guess what? Lo and behold, a businessman from the United Kingdom replied to the ad within an hour. (Kudos to Craigslist!) He was excited and asked to see the house as soon as possible.

Gulp. *Breathe in. Breathe out.*

"I love the house," he said after a brief tour the day after I posted the ad. "And I'm ready to sign the lease and give you a check. But I have one request: My wife and I and our young child need to move in by this Friday."

"Wait. This Friday? As in two days?"

"Yes, this Friday. If you can't make it happen, we'll have to look at other options."

Double gulp. *Breathe in. Breathe out.*

You can probably imagine the difficult conversation I had with my wife that evening. She was on board with living a life of obedience to Christ and pursuing our convictions, but to allow strangers to move into our home, to move out with our kids and go "couch surfing" for ten weeks, and to make this decision in two days?

Yes, there were some glares, elevated voices, and there may or may not have been a tear or two, or several. Even then, we both prayed about it and agreed to move forward.

At that moment, I came to a deeper and more painful realization of something that was becoming evident. I was more enamored with the *idea* of changing the world and less enamored with actually doing it. I didn't want to leave my comfort for the sake of my commitments.

God, this is not what I signed up for. In my mind, I questioned God and I questioned myself: *How did it ever come to this?*

A Conviction

Two years prior to this family meeting, I found myself in a village in a remote area of the jungle in Myanmar (otherwise known as Burma). United Nations officials had deemed the genocide in certain parts of Burma as equal to if not worse than that of the crisis in Darfur in the 1990s—but it had been widely forgotten in the global media.

On that trip I visited a makeshift school that sat in the middle of the jungle. It was obviously unlike any of the schools my children attend.

Imagine a shack, with old wooden desks and chairs, overused by a couple of decades, and a deeply scratched-up chalkboard. When I walked into the classroom—meant for about fifteen first through fifth graders—the desks, chairs, and chalkboard weren't really what caught my attention. Rather, it was a poster taped on the chalkboard that captured me, because, to put it bluntly, it was disgusting—unlike anything I have ever seen.

The poster featured a collage of photos of numerous men, women, and children with missing limbs. A few photos showed, in graphic detail, oozing, bloody body parts. I'm not a teacher and have no experience with what should or should not be placed on the walls of a typical classroom, but this was clearly inappropriate.

I tried to remain unfazed, but when my hosts from this village sensed my horror, they invited me to step up to the chalkboard and have a closer look at the poster. With reluctance, I took a couple of steps closer, and it was then that my host pointed to the bottom of the poster.

"Pastor Cho. These"—he pointed to a row of greenish contraptions—"are land mines. We must teach our children how to avoid land mines."

My mind blown.

My heart wrecked.

Take a moment and let this story sink in …

Forty Dollars?

Later, in conversation with one of the village elders, I learned of their many challenges as a result of living in constant fear of their oppressive military government. This government has been known by many in the global community for its reputation of suppressing dissent and perpetuating human-rights abuses, and its persecution of minority ethnic groups in Burma, including the Karen people.

This village—comprising mostly Karen internally displaced refugees, or IDPs—like many others, didn't even have a name because its residents often had to pack up quickly to flee when they heard news of an imminent government attack; the village was simply designated by a number. Despite the hardships and challenges the villagers faced, I was genuinely compelled by their sense of hope and courage.

I asked, "What are your biggest challenges?"

"Schools. Teachers. Paying teachers hard," replied one of the village elders in broken English, knowing that I had visited one of their makeshift schools earlier in the day.

The school couldn't hold on to its teachers because they kept leaving to take jobs across the border in Thailand, where schools offered higher salaries. Out of curiosity, I asked this village elder about the salary of their teachers.

"About forty dollars," he responded.

Without even thinking, I replied, "Forty dollars a day?"

He laughed and then shook his head.

Embarrassed, I said, "I'm sorry. Forty dollars a week?"

There was no laugh this time. He just shook his head. What? Oh my goodness. How could their salaries be forty dollars per month?

"Forty dollars a month?" I asked.

While I expected an affirmation, the elder shook his head again, and I couldn't fathom the possibility of my next guess being accurate.

With hesitation and incredulity, I asked, "Forty dollars a year?" And he finally nodded his head.

Forty dollars a year!

I couldn't believe it. That's what I'd spend on a cheap date night with my wife, a few books, a cell phone bill, or a tank of gas. But forty dollars prevented this village from keeping their teachers around.

To some degree, I shouldn't have been surprised. I already knew about global poverty, knew the numbers, knew them by heart, in fact, because I memorized many of them for the talks I did at churches, universities, and conferences. But now that I was seeing the people behind the statistics, it wrecked me.

We couldn't sit around and go back to life as usual. Convicted and moved, Minhee and I decided we had to do something. We would ask people to give up what they earned for just one day's work—about 0.4 percent of their annual salary—and that money would change lives in real ways. This became One Day's Wages (ODW), a grassroots movement of people, stories, and action to alleviate extreme global poverty.

However, this wasn't just about starting something. It wasn't just about doing something. There was more. By far, more dangerous and uncomfortable. God was challenging us not just to "change the world"; He was inviting *us* to change. You see, it's easier to talk about wanting to change the world; to talk about the need to change this and change that; to start this movement and start that organization. But if I'm honest, we don't always do it, and we don't always want to think that we, ourselves, have to change in the process.

This notion is succinctly captured by a quote from nineteenth-century Russian novelist Leo Tolstoy:

> Everyone thinks of changing the world, but no one
> thinks of changing himself.

As Minhee and I spent time discussing how to respond to the convictions of our hearts, we prayed for direction, vision, and clarity.

What we sensed was not pleasant. Not pleasant at all. At least for me. It wasn't what I had in mind. Maybe I could craft a nice thirty-minute sermon, write a series of blog posts, or recommend books and links for people to check out on Facebook. But isn't that what makes discipleship so uncomfortable and challenging? God often leads us on journeys we would never go on if it were up to us. It's our ideas versus God's will. It's our agendas versus God's will. It's our plans versus God's will.

In prayer, both Minhee and I sensed an invitation from the Holy Spirit to give up an entire year's salary. Minhee was then a homemaker and thus the CEO of the Cho clan, and I am a full-time pastor. Our yearly salary was $68,000.

Now, I'll share more about this in the next chapter, but let me just make this clear. It's not an easy admission a pastor—apart from perhaps a prosperity theology pastor—should make, but here it is: *I like my money.*

There, I said it.

Also, I like my stuff. I like upgrading things. I feel as though I've earned my paycheck. I pride myself in caring for and providing for my family. These are the reasons why this conviction was so challenging and uncomfortable.

Thus our journey began, but I began this quest, in part, because I sensed *I could do it.* However, Minhee and I had no idea exactly how difficult this conviction would be to live out.

Since we didn't have $68,000 in cash stashed under our mattress or in an offshore Cayman account, we began what eventually became a three-year journey. We made a family decision to buy only essentials and groceries. We decided to put on hold things such as piano lessons for our children. (Thankfully, our kids aren't musical prodigies!) Soccer and basketball camps were put on hiatus. Minhee gave up shopping for clothing and accessories. And since we're being honest, I gave up my accessories too. I had to part with my midlife crisis car, which I referred to as "Blue Thunder"—my 1991 Mazda Miata, painted radiant blue. And yes, I really did call it Blue Thunder. I'll share more about the legend of this car in the next chapter.

So after nearly three laborious years of scraping and saving, we were still short $10,000. And that leads me back to the story of the Craigslist ad.

We had only a few months left on the timetable to come up with the total sum. We deliberated. We prayed. We fasted. We talked. We sought counsel. We went for many walks. *What should we do? Take a little more time?*

We had done our best; that was good enough, right? But the Holy Spirit kept prompting us forward. While we were emotionally drained and at times experienced doubt and questioned our sanity, we sensed the Holy Spirit pushing us to be faithful and honor the convictions we clearly sensed from God three years prior. In short, we sensed God exhorting us to not quit, to remain steadfast and tenacious, and that God was not yet done with us. Clinging on to only these things, Minhee and I sat down with the kids. We told them we had decided to sublet our home, not for the eight weeks that I had initially advertised on Craigslist but for ten weeks, and that within forty-eight hours, we would pack up a few things and stay with some friends.

Our instructions to ourselves and our children were simple:

> Everyone gets to pack one bag. Pack your essential
> clothes, a couple of books, and, kids, you can take
> your favorite toy. One bag.

The night I told our kids about the plan, I did my best to remain composed and in control. Later that evening, after our nightly family prayer and after tucking the kids into their beds, I could no longer stay composed. In the privacy of my office, I wept like a baby. This wasn't what I'd signed up for. I couldn't believe that at the age of thirty-eight, I had placed my wife and children in this situation.

I felt as if I'd failed my family and that I was the worst husband and father; a deadbeat; an absolute failure.

Needless to say, it was a humbling moment. Had I foreseen it, there is no way in hades I would have gone forward with our pledge. It really is God's grace that He doesn't reveal the entirety of our futures all at once. If we knew what we'd have to face in the future, we'd all likely run the other way—like Jonah.

Our family spent the next ten weeks with friends, staying in guest rooms and on couches. Though we were a little embarrassed and bruised, I was reminded that our hope was not in a vision, a donor, a website, an idea, or a strategy, but in the Lord Himself. Our hope was in the Lord who loves my family more than I could ever imagine.

What I learned (again!) is that despite our best-laid plans and intentions, things don't always work out the way we envision—and that's okay. God is in control. His love for us does not waver. If anything, God loves us so profoundly that He's willing to journey with us through our deserts and valleys so that we become more defined and refined in His purposes and character.

We live in a world and culture in which—both out of privilege and conviction—many want to make an impact.

It is true: Many want to *change the world.*

The statistics prove only that we are living among generations—in a time, context, and culture—who want to make a difference. As such, I often hear our generations being heralded: "This is the generation that will accomplish something extraordinary." Praises such as "game changers," "history makers," and "world changers" are lavished upon people. I suspect that versions of such statements have been said of generations past and will be said of future generations as well.

Truthfully, these statements make for good motivational talks. They make for good sermons and conference speeches.

But let's take a moment to pause.

We need to be wise.

We need to pray for wisdom.

We need to engage a posture of humility.

While I want to applaud (really!) the desire and sincerity of people wanting to change the world, I fear that if we're not careful, we might become … *the most overrated generation.*

I fear that we might be more in love with the idea of changing the world than *actually* changing the world.

I fear that we might be more enamored with the *idea* of changing the world and are neglecting to allow ourselves to be changed.

I fear that we have an unrealistic and glamorous perception of what it means to follow Christ and what it means to pursue justice. In truth, we have not taken the time to count the costs of following Jesus.

I fear that we might be tempted to compartmentalize the action of changing the world rather than seeing it as a key part of our discipleship journey that will impact the whole of our lives.

I fear that we're asking God to move mountains, forgetting that God also wants to move us. And in fact, it may be possible that *we* are the mountains that need to be moved.

We live in extraordinary times. Those of us in the Western world live with extraordinary resources and privileges. In Luke 12:48, we're given these words of truth: "From everyone who has been given much, much will be demanded."

We have been given much. Approximately 80 percent of the world lives on less than ten American dollars a day, so by comparison, most of us are part of the richest 1 percent in the world.

But it's not just wealth. We have resources, access, and the privilege of vast opportunities. We live in a context where we can entertain, explore, and pray through career choices, options, entrepreneurial thoughts, and business ideas.

Yet I think our wealth of resources and opportunities lends itself to this theory that we may be part of the most overrated generation in human history—because we have access to so much data, info, resources, modes of communication … but we end up doing so little. We tweet, blog, talk, preach, retweet, share, like, and click incessantly. While I'm not implying that the aforementioned things aren't actions, what do those actions actually cost us? How are we sacrificing? In fact, recent research even indicates that people who demonstrate support for causes and organizations on social media, such as Facebook, actually do less in real life. They are less likely to donate their money or volunteer their time.

> Researchers at the University of British Columbia compared how volunteers behaved after public displays of support (like Facebook liking and pin-wearing) and private actions (like signing a petition). People making public displays were less likely to donate money or time at a later date.[1]

So, I ask again:

How are we truly changing the world?

How are we deeply engaging in what God is already doing in the world?

How are we listening to the Holy Spirit?

And how are we being changed ourselves?

How am I being changed?

I am a preacher.

I am a teacher.

I am a blogger and writer.

I am a public speaker.

Over the years I've gained a reputation of being deeply passionate about justice, mercy, and compassion; of being an agent of change, a catalyst of justice.

And that's what I convinced myself too. In other words, I believed in what people were saying of me. I believed in my own hype.

It wasn't until this surprising season of my life that I arrived at an incredibly painful realization that while my heart might have had good intentions, I was more in love with the *idea* of changing the world.

Is this perhaps your confession too?

Chapter 2

WHY WE DO JUSTICE

The topic of justice is expansive. One can write many volumes solely dedicated to this important issue. I want to share about the importance of justice, as well as the dangers of justice apart from grounding it in the gospel.

I love justice.

Justice is cool.

Justice is glamorous.

Justice is heroic.

Pursuing justice makes me feel important.

Pursuing justice makes me feel good.

It makes me feel heroic.

I like talking about justice.

I like writing about justice.

And perhaps I'm not alone in these thoughts and confessions.

In fact, I believe that most people—particularly followers of Jesus—love justice. Right? We all love justice … until there's a cost.

But here's the tension and truth: There's always a cost to doing justice. And there's always a cost to following Jesus.

And for all the reasons above, and for reasons I've not listed, we need to know what justice is and why we engage in the pursuit of justice, and we need to have the courage to examine how we do this work of justice.

Justice can be a loaded word to Christians, speaking to their hearts and passions, or speaking to their fears. Christians who've yet to understand the importance of justice sometimes categorize justice as irrelevant, isolated, or a current cultural fad.

Since some contend we are at a historical apex in the pursuit of justice, and others contend justice has become more trendy than substantive, the truth may lie somewhere in the middle. But that doesn't take away from the fact that justice is very important.

However, I am convinced that even the important topic, and pursuit, of justice—apart from the gospel of Christ—can grow to be idolatrous. So, let's take a chapter to explain why justice is not isolated or irrelevant but is instead a central and critical aspect of God's character and the gospel.

Who Is Justice?

You cannot read the Scriptures without sensing God's heart for justice. It is pervasive throughout the Bible. In fact, the Hebrew word for justice appears "more than two hundred times" throughout just the Old Testament.[1] We see God's love for the widow, orphan, immigrant, and the poor. We see God's love for the marginalized, oppressed, and forgotten.

Learn to do right; seek justice.
>	Defend the oppressed.
Take up the cause of the fatherless;
>	plead the case of the widow. (Isa. 1:17)

He has shown you, O mortal, what is good.
>	And what does the LORD require of you?
To act justly and to love mercy
>	and to walk humbly with your God. (Mic. 6:8)

This is what the LORD says: Do what is just and right. Rescue from the hand of the oppressor the one who has been robbed. Do no wrong or violence to the foreigner, the fatherless or the widow, and do no shed innocent blood in this place. (Jer. 22:3)

The LORD loves righteousness and justice;
>	the earth is full of his unfailing love. (Ps. 33:5)

Blessed are those who act justly,
>	who always do what is right. (Ps. 106:3)

Follow justice and justice alone, so that you may live and possess the land the LORD your God is giving you. (Deut. 16:20)

I know that the LORD secures justice for the poor
>	and upholds the cause of the needy. (Ps. 140:12)

> Yet the LORD longs to be gracious to you;
>> therefore he will rise up to show you
>>> compassion.
> For the LORD is a God of justice. (Isa. 30:18)

The list of scriptures that speak to God's love for justice goes on and on. The theme of justice is not merely peppered into the Bible here and there; it is woven throughout the narrative of God's story. Justice is not peripheral but rather is central to God's story.

Ken Wytsma, author of *Pursuing Justice*, helps us with a beautiful working definition of justice that can be claimed by both the church and culture:

> *Justice* is the single best word, both inside and out-side the Bible, for capturing God's purposes for the world and humanity's calling in the world. *Justice* is, in fact, the broadest, most consistent word the Bible uses to speak about *what ought to be*, and it has been used throughout the centuries by Christians and non-Christians alike to describe vital areas of human and divine concern.[2]

So, what does it mean to engage in the work of justice according to Wytsma?

> To "do justice" means to render to each what each is due. Justice involves harmony, flourishing, and fair-ness, and it is based on the image of God in every

person—the *Imago Dei*—that grants all people inalienable dignity and infinite worth.[3]

Or to simplify that definition: "Justice is doing for others what we would want done for us."[4]

Amen and amen.

Justice is the act of restoring something to fullness after it has been harmed. Justice is making things right. But that definition for me is still a little incomplete. Even more fundamental than a definition of justice is the place from which our understanding of justice emanates. It is hard to restore what has been wronged if you don't have a point of reference. We need to know what this fullness looks like in its pure form. We need to know where this restoration comes from. If fullness is the goal for us as the church and as Christians, we must seek to understand the fullness of what God intended for His creation. We need to more deeply understand God the Father, Jesus the Son of God, and the Holy Spirit. We need to more deeply grow in intimacy with the Creator, Redeemer, and Sustainer. More often than not, we're fixed in the brokenness of our world because we are constantly surrounded by such things. But if we're not careful, we lose sight of God. We lose sight of God's purposes and intent for creation. We lose sight of God's promise to restore our brokenness and our fallen world.

This is why for us, as Christians, the person of God, the deity of God, God's justice, and God's goodness are such powerful things. God's justice is His plan of redemption for a broken world. God's justice is renewing the world to where He would have intended it to be.

Justice is not just a thing that is good. Justice is not merely doing good. Justice is not something that's moral or right or fair. Justice is not, in itself, a set of ethics. Justice is not just an aggregation of the many justice-themed verses throughout the Scriptures. Justice is not trendy, glamorous, cool, or sexy. Justice isn't a movement. Justice is so much more, and the understanding of this fullness is central to the work that we do in pursuing justice.

What Is Justice?

To more thoroughly understand justice, we must reflect on the truth that justice is a reflection of God's character. Justice is the pursuit of the shalom that God intended for the world and humanity. And for this reason, we read again and again in the Scriptures that God is just and that God loves justice. They are inseparable. In the same way we shouldn't isolate or extract love or holiness from God's character, such must be the case for justice. Such is the reality.

Our God is just.

Our God loves justice.

And the people of God should love what and whom God loves.

God invites and commands His people to not just be aware of injustice but to pursue justice. Not just to pursue justice but to *live justly*. These two acts are not the same, but they are inseparable. To be followers of Jesus, we are required to pursue justice and live justly at the same time. This is a truth that ought to inform both our theology of justice and our praxis of justice (how we live out our faith in the world), and we seek to live this way because, ultimately, justice reflects the character of God. We do justice because justice is rooted in the character of God and thus must reflect in the character of His followers.

Jesus Versus Justice?

Why is it that so many in the church still seek to lower the importance of justice in the order of things in God's kingdom? Why are so many still seeking to separate or distinguish Jesus from a godly pursuit of justice?

I get questions such as these all the time:

> Why do you care so much about justice? Why can't you just focus on Jesus?

Or my favorite:

> If you are a Christian, why do you need to be concerned about this justice business? All you have to do is focus on Jesus. It's all about Jesus. Just focus on Jesus.

Some in the church throw out an either/or scenario: The binary worldview that is the Jesus versus justice debate. Why can't a Christ follower pursue both? Some imply that a Christ follower is supposed to sacrifice one for the other.

Don't get lost in this debate. It's a false dichotomy.

I respond, shaking my fist in the air, "We *are* focusing on Jesus!" (Okay, maybe no fist shaking.) Jesus cared about people. He stood with people in their times of need. I can give biblical example after biblical example showing how He lived with people and loved them.

Jesus loves justice. And justice, by its very nature, involves people. I've learned that people often struggle with Jesus's commitment to justice because He rarely, if ever, spelled out the importance of justice in a three-point sermon.

Instead, Jesus lived justly.

Justice was in Jesus.

He reflected justice in how He lived, how He loved, and how He welcomed the stranger, the marginalized, the leper, the widow, the prostitute, and the sick. Jesus reflected justice in how He approached the powers and systems of His age, how He confronted religious leaders, how He embraced, welcomed, and empowered women, and how He confronted ethnic biases and prejudices.

Yes, Jesus loved justice, but more so, He lived justly. And here's the truth: He calls us to follow Him.

I get my share of emails and letters. Not many cookies, but plenty of emails and letters from strangers near and far seeking to rebuke me and restore me to the narrow path. I even get occasional pamphlets on the Four Spiritual Laws and other nice Bible tracts.

Here's an example of a common email:

Dear Pastor Eugene,

I admire your work at One Day's Wages and highly respect your ministry. I just wanted to encourage you with a different perspective on your passion for social justice.

I can tell your passion comes from good intentions and out of "righteous anger" from your perspective. But I and many other believers may think differently from you. It distracts me greatly to see your opinions on current affairs instead of God's goodness and on His Word.

There are many important reasons to be aware of social justice issues, but I believe the Lord has ordained you to take on the greater role as a pastor, whose utmost duty is to preach the Word and to be used as an instrument to save souls.

I think it will be good for you to examine how balanced you are in your passion for talking about God's goodness and His actual Word, compared to your passion for social justice. Those of us who care for you want to see you focus more on Jesus, if you can understand that at all.

If you feel that you are truly led by the Holy Spirit to deal with our justice system, I would like to encourage you to do that as a full-time career. In fact, I think you will be excellent because I know you are a passionate person. But to have a title of pastor and to focus so much on evening news topics is truly not only distracting but dividing as well.

Sincerely,
NAME

Why Do I Care About Justice?

I care about justice because I care about the gospel.

I care about Jesus.

I care about the kingdom of God.

The pursuit of justice cannot stand alone for followers of Jesus. For Christians, the gospel informs everything we do—including our understanding and praxis of justice.

In other words, the most important aspect of the kingdom of God is not justice as some have contended it is. The most important thing about the kingdom of God … is the kingdom of God. The most important thing about the kingdom of God … is the gospel. Jesus came to usher in the kingdom of God, and part of the promise of the gospel is that Jesus came to reconcile and restore all that is good and beautiful back unto the One.

If you truly believe in the gospel of Jesus Christ, then you believe that the gospel matters not just for your personal salvation and blessing, but also for God's pursuit of restoration, redemption, and reconciliation of the entire world.

Christians believe in the gospel that is revealed to us in the life, death, and resurrection of Christ:

> A gospel that not only saves but also serves;
> A gospel that not only saves but seeks to restore all
>   things back unto the One that ushered forth
>   all that is good and beautiful;
> A gospel that not only saves but ushers in the
>   kingdom of God;
> A gospel that not only saves but restores the
>   dignity of humanity—even in the midst of
>   our brokenness and depravity.

This gospel is not just for us. The gospel is good news for all.

Justice as Discipleship

You will know a tree from its fruit.

In other words, you will show evidence of where you are rooted if you produce fruit that is close to the heart of God. To that end, I believe you cannot credibly follow Christ unless you pursue justice.

I know that a lot of people will push back on that statement. Some say that salvation hinges on whether or not you believe in Jesus, and that is true. But do you really believe in Jesus when there is no evidence that you are doing what He compels us to do?

Early in Jesus's ministry, He boldly proclaimed His revolutionary vision for the kingdom of God in a synagogue on the Sabbath, and the religious authorities surrounding Him stood amazed at His teaching. He stood up to read, and someone handed Him a scroll of the prophet Isaiah.

He found these defining words and read them:

> The Spirit of the Lord is on me,
>   because he has anointed me
>   to proclaim good news to the poor.
> He has sent me to proclaim freedom for the
>   prisoners
>   and recovery of sight for the blind,
> to set the oppressed free,
>   to proclaim the year of the Lord's favor.
>   (Luke 4:18–19)

Thy kingdom come. Thy will be done. On earth as it is in heaven.

This was a proclamation of justice for the poor, the blind, and the prisoner, fulfilling a kingdom vision that included "the least of these." A kingdom vision that even His closest disciples did not fully understand at the time. Shortly after this time, Jesus was rejected.

There was confusion. There was anger. The religious leaders listening to Jesus got angry, and their curiosity and amazement turned to apprehension, even fear. They believed that this humble arrival of the King was not how it was supposed to be.

So an angry mob chased Him out of town and tried to run Him off a cliff (see Luke 4:29).

Biblical justice often does not make sense from our human perspective: The last shall become first. The weak will become strong. The poor will become rich.

What paradoxes!

How can you read the Scriptures or examine the life and ministry of Christ and not sense that mercy, justice, and compassion—particularly for those who have been marginalized—aren't dear to the heart of God?

When we read through the Bible, it is clear to me that God cares about justice. The Word of God is God's revelation for the world, showing how the world can be set right. We see that Jesus is not some mere historical figure—Jesus is the Son of God; He is God incarnate. His words and actions testify to the kingdom of God, where things will be restored, where there is justice, mercy, and compassion.

All of this matters because we are not just talking about ideas. We are not just hypothesizing about a "what if" scenario. This matters because justice involves people and their lives and their value before God. When justice happens to the least of these, God celebrates.

As Christians, we know and understand justice beyond secular definitions. It is not peripheral. It is not external. It is not secondary. It is critical. It is part of our identities. It is part of our discipleship. It is an important part of our witness to the world.

Even the Most Loyal Miss It

I can't think of anyone who was more excited or prepared for the arrival of Jesus than John the Baptist. The whole purpose of his life was to prepare the way for the Lord: "He must become greater; I must become less" (John 3:30).

What I find so fascinating about John the Baptist is that he had prepared for so long. And then when Jesus came, he began to have doubts because of how Jesus lived. You find John the Baptist in jail, anticipating that his days were numbered, thinking, *Is Jesus the One? I've got to know.*

He sent his disciples to ask Jesus that very question: "Are you the one who is to come, or should we expect someone else?" (Luke 7:20). And it blows my mind, because here is a guy who devoted his whole adult life to prepare the way for Jesus.

To proclaim the Savior.

To know the Savior.

He doubted Jesus because the way He conducted His ministry was different from what John had imagined. I suspect John the Baptist envisioned Jesus doing what he was doing, but on a bigger scale: Bigger audiences. More sermons. Louder voice with sound effects. Multisite venues. More miracles and baptisms. More of everything. He probably imagined Jesus cracking some heads and taking some names: "The kingdom of God has come near. Repent and believe the good news!" (Mark 1:15).

Now, Jesus *does* tell people to repent, to reconcile with God. But when John asked his question about the Savior's identity at this moment of crisis in prison, Jesus answered in a way that vividly shows the depth, height, width, and heart of the gospel:

When the men came to Jesus, they said, "John the Baptist sent us to you to ask, 'Are you the one who is to come, or should we expect someone else?'"

At that very time Jesus cured many who had diseases, sicknesses and evil spirits, and gave sight to many who were blind. So he replied to the messengers, "Go back and report to John what you have seen and heard: The blind receive sight, the lame walk, those who have leprosy are cleansed, the deaf hear, the dead are raised, and the good news is proclaimed to the poor." (Luke 7:20–22)

As I see it, this is the fullness of the scandalous and profound beauty of the gospel. This is a gospel that proclaims God's love for all people, including and especially those who have been forgotten in our society, and dare I say it, perhaps even in our churches.

This is the gospel lived out. It's not just about the Four Spiritual Laws or lofty theology. This, simply put, is hope for those with no hope.

This is action.

This is Jesus.

If this understanding of the gospel is what informs our understanding of social justice, I'm all for it. Or in proper Christian vernacular, social justice means to love your neighbor. To serve, advocate, and care for a more just society. *Mishpat*, a Hebrew word used in the Old Testament for justice, literally means "to treat people equitably" or "to give people their rights."[5] So it's the *mishpat* way of following God.

Tim Keller, in his book *Generous Justice*, speaks eloquently to this point:

It is also impossible to separate word and deed ministry from each other in ministry because human beings are integrated wholes—body and soul. When some Christians say, "Caring for physical needs will detract from evangelism," they must be thinking only of doing evangelism among people who are comfortable and well-off.[6]

In the pursuit of justice, we cannot divorce the spiritual from the physical. Justice wasn't meant to be compartmentalized in this way. As followers of the living God who acts on this earth through His people, we must pursue justice. The gospel of Jesus, the kingdom vision, should inform and inspire those in authority to a better way of living.

The life of Martin Luther King Jr. was one that typified the pursuit of justice, both spiritually and socially. He said these words:

A religion true to its nature must also be concerned about man's social conditions.... Any religion that professes to be concerned with the souls of men and is not concerned with the slums that damn them, the economic conditions that strangle them, and the social conditions that cripple them is a dry-as-dust religion.[7]

Justice as Evangelism

Christians should not just engage with other Christians. God calls us to be light to the world, not merely light to the light. As a result, we are going to engage other people with other worldviews. In fact, we *have to* engage people with other worldviews. Not only is this okay, but this is good.

I believe for social justice to work in a Christian context, we must be ready to share why we act, why we live justly. There are those who have grown so timid about their faith that they won't engage in that conversation at all. This also is detrimental to the witness of Christ.

Doing good is beautiful, but let's pray that doing good provokes, evokes, and fascinates people toward the gospel, prompting them to ask of you or me:

Who are you?
What are you about?
What compels you to do what you do?

As Christians, we should be excited and ready to respond to such questions, in the hope that people may be drawn to Jesus. But let's not go to the other extreme: We should not serve on the condition that recipients behave the way we deem right, or make our services contingent on someone's theological and spiritual convictions. That is a distorted twenty-first-century version of colonialism.

My motto in life is "Live what you say. Say what you live."

I am so grateful that, while One Day's Wages is not legally a Christian organization, our faith in Christ is what birthed and sustains our work. I cannot help but joyfully share about the manner in which this organization was formed. One Day's Wages exists because Minhee and I felt God's conviction in our hearts and followed God's heart for compassion, mercy, and justice.

I have had the opportunity to share about the birth of One Day's Wages at numerous conferences and secular institutions, and when I relay this story, one reaction is common. People will come up to me and tell me, "I will probably never go to church. But if I did, I'd go to your church." Others tell me, "I left the church years ago. But you have made me think about Jesus all over again." I hear this again and again.

They say they'll never come. I can only smile and give glory to Christ when a couple of them start coming to the church I pastor, or when they send me a note from afar saying that they've renewed their relationship with God. This is grace, and we're grateful for the opportunity—in all our imperfections—to be a witness for God's glorious grace and love.

What does evangelism look like in our current context?

The people in the New Testament book of Acts were hearing about Jesus for the very first time. Today we're dealing with a generation in which nearly everyone has heard about Jesus in some way. While it's true that what people have heard is often distorted, we can't dismiss that many have a negative feeling toward Jesus, particularly toward His followers. So how do we speak to a culture and world that have a broken and false understanding of Jesus?

In my years of living in Seattle, I have never met anyone who has not heard of Jesus Christ. They know Jesus, or more accurately, they think they know of Jesus. They have an opinion, one way or another. What they believe may not be true or consistent to the Jesus who loved unconditionally, sought peace, pursued the marginalized and poor, and challenged unjust structures and systems.

What brings credibility to the gospel is not more hour-long sermons. What brings credibility, passion, and, ultimately, belief is seeing the gospel at work … the incarnate gospel.

What will move skeptics, cynics, and critics are Christians who love God and love their neighbors—including neighbors who don't look like them—by willingly and humbly serving their needs.

Tim Keller emphasizes this point in *Generous Justice*:

> We instinctively tend to limit for whom we exert ourselves. We do it for people like us, and for people whom we like. Jesus will have none of that. By depicting a Samaritan helping a Jew, Jesus could not have found a more forceful way to say that anyone at all in need—regardless of race, politics, class, and religion—is your neighbor. Not everyone is your brother or sister in the faith, but everyone is your neighbor, and you must love your neighbor.[8]

Want to compel the skeptics, cynics, and critics of Christianity? When they see Christians who care about justice in our broken world, that's compelling! Seeking justice, loving mercy, and walking humbly brings more credibility to our faith as we seek to represent the way of Jesus. Justice matters because God cares about justice; justice matters to victims of injustice; and ultimately, justice is important in our evangelism.

Live what you say.

Say what you live.

Certainly, justice is not the totality of our evangelism, but with justice comes credibility and trust.

Justice Does Us

Everyone loves the idea of justice until there is a cost. Ironically, justice is never convenient, and there is always a cost. This is why we often like "doing justice" or following Jesus up to the point at which it provokes an act of sacrifice, forcing us to change the way we live or change the way we think.

In some part, this is why it's difficult for me to share the story of One Day's Wages without challenging our dominant worldviews and the way we live our lives. For my wife and me, God challenged us to live more simply. He challenged us to give up some of the excess in our lives.

In seeking to do justice, we have to be open to the reality that God will challenge us, change us, and transform us. In doing justice and in doing things that matter to God, we actually grow more in His likeness. We will begin to reflect more of the character of God. We grow more intimate with the heart of God.

We will do things because they embody the kingdom of God. And it is right in the eyes of God. But in doing these things, there is something equally beautiful, in that we become more in tune with the heart of God.

Oftentimes, we go about our concept of justice or compassion or generosity when it is about us and our power and privilege to do something for others, without entertaining the possibility that maybe God wants to change us.

We have much to learn from the poor, marginalized, and oppressed. We have much to learn from those in the developing world. We have much to learn from those in the inner cities. We have much to learn from our neighbors who do not look like us, think like us, or act like us. We may even have much to learn from our enemies. There is a level of humility that justice exacts inside us.

God's heart for justice is an expression of grace itself. God hasn't given up on His creation. God hasn't given up on the world. God hasn't given up on you. The truth is that He calls His church to pursue justice, to right wrongs, and to proclaim good news to the poor. How can we not believe in this kind of gospel … when this gospel has been extended to us?

The inescapable truth about justice is that there is something wrong in the world that needs to be set right. Sometimes the things that need to be set right are not just in the lives of those we seek to serve. The things that need to be set right may also be in our own lives.

We need to pursue justice not just because the world is broken, but because we're broken too. Pursuing justice helps us put our own lives in order. Perhaps this is what God intended—that in doing His work serving others, we discover more of His character and are changed ourselves.

The following chapters describe some of the ways in which that has taken place in my life. Ironically, in my spiritual attempts to "change the world," I learned how much *I* needed to change. As I sought to do justice, God sought to change me.

Chapter 3

THE TENSION OF UPWARD MOBILITY: WE ARE BLESSED

I will never forget Blue Thunder.

Most of us have some kind of worldly, materialistic obsession. We all struggle with our stuff. And if you say that you don't, perhaps you struggle with lying. Maybe it's designer shoes or high-end handbags or the newest TV or the smallest Apple iAnything. Maybe it's *Star Wars* figurines. (No judgment there. My son's name is Jedi, and I personally own two *Star Wars* bobbleheads.)

But for me, I have diagnosed my Achilles' heel: *convertibles*.

I've managed to rationalize having three convertibles in the two decades I have been driving. I blame my father, who started this obsession by buying me a very beat-up 1976 Volkswagen Beetle convertible. Yes, the car was orange, and no, it didn't have functioning seat belts, but whatever. My favorite convertible by far, however, was Blue Thunder.

What or who is Blue Thunder?

It was my midlife-crisis car. Several years ago, I traded in our family's reliable-at-first-then-unreliable Toyota Camry station wagon and brought home a 1990 Mazda Miata (its first production year).

New wheels, a functioning soft top, and an almost flawless bright blue paint job. Blue Thunder and I used to spend quality time cruising through Seattle and the great Northwest with my curly Asian locks flowing in the wind—especially during those rare but oh-so-sweet sunny days.

It was love. Oh, my beautiful Baby Blue. Yes, midlife crisis indeed.

"Don't worry, Minhee. I'll make sure I trade in our station wagon for another practical family automobile."

When I drove the Miata home to show Minhee, you should've seen the look on her face—because getting a two-seater convertible was probably the furthest thing from her mind; it was priceless. #BestHusbandEver

So for a guy who seeks to live a life of simplicity, you can see how this could result in some tension. Especially when we bought a used sedan to aid our minivan in hauling the kids around and the Miata became a third car.

At that point we really didn't need it. It often sat idle for weeks, though we would lend it to folks who needed a ride for a few days. But that didn't mean I didn't want it. I just wanted to keep it for myself, look at it, and cruise around in it. Heck, if I could have worn Blue Thunder as a necklace and called it My Precious, I would have.

Sweet Blue Thunder.

To be honest with you, I may have a problem. I call it … car porn. Every time I enter a bookstore, I make a beeline to the magazine rack and look for the automobile magazines. "Cultural research and exegesis," I tell my wife. Ogling the lines of the Italian exotics, the glamorous German masters of the autobahn … and my oh my, those convertibles.

Did I mention I like convertibles?

So here's where my obsession started to unravel.

When Minhee and I decided to start One Day's Wages, we made a public pledge to donate a year's salary to the organization. Keeping that pledge was more difficult than we could have ever imagined (as I explained in chapter 1), but we agreed that selling many of our things was important. Part of our plan was to sell Blue Thunder.

So I reluctantly placed an ad for the Miata on Craigslist. Me and Craigslist. Craigslist and me. We're like best friends. Anyway, my wife and I (emphasis more on my wife) decided that we had to sell the Miata in order to reach our goal. People came to see it, and some offers came in, but no one followed through with the purchase. Minhee was disappointed, but I was dancing and singing, wearing a linen ephod a la King David. I couldn't have been happier that it didn't sell, because let's be honest, we all like our stuff.

Then some dude came to see the car, loved it, and agreed to pay full price. I bought the car for $3,100 and ended up selling it for $3,200. What a jerk! It rocked my world when Blue Thunder drove away. My heart sank. And I wish I was kidding.

Melodramatic stories aside, what surprised me most was how bad I felt for myself. God had blessed us with so much, and I couldn't even follow through on some basic convictions without feeling pity for myself.

Perhaps I'm not alone. Perhaps I'm like everyone else. I like my stuff. We all like toys, cards, stuff, and gadgets. I don't want to knock it and say that we can't enjoy life, but at what point do we say, "Enough is enough"?

For me, the Miata became an example of fun, but also excess. It became a challenge for me to let go of Blue Thunder because I was wrestling with full knowledge of the level of poverty in the rest of the world. Still, I didn't want to give it up. I can't speak for you, but I do know that God had been prompting me to live more generously, and I was resisting. I placed more value on my stuff than on the convictions God had placed on my heart.

Generosity is what keeps the things I own from owning me. In other words, the point of my generosity isn't just to bless others; it's also to liberate me.

Now this is sad, and it's embarrassing to admit: I may or may not have teared up a little on the day I sold Blue Thunder. So that's why I wrote this, half in jest, half in truth:

Dear Baby Blue:
I'll miss you. We had good times.
You never broke down. Never.
True, you got broken into twice
but you kept running well.
I enjoyed putting your top town and
letting my long curly Asian hair blow
through the Seattle skyline.
So, I will miss you but when it's all
said and done, you're just a car.

You are what you are. Nothing more.

Take care and who knows?

When the kids are all out of the house,

maybe I'll shock Minhee one more time

by exchanging our family van for a …

Beware of Mammon

I say this all the time: "Be generous. Live lives of radical generosity." I know this, think this, preach this, teach this, blog this, tell people this, am committed to this, and believe this idea of "being generous" is a critical part of our discipleship. And I hope you do too.

Ah … but it's easier said than done. And even easier tweeted than done.

So what prevents us from radical generosity?

The answer is both simple and complex: mammon.

Mammon means "material wealth or greed," especially when we elevate this wealth into a godlike status.[1] That's a fancy way of saying "idolatry." We harbor an often-unacknowledged, idolatrous love of money. That is dangerous, because money—if it becomes an idol in our lives—becomes a legitimate competitor to the lordship of God.

In my reading of the Scriptures, the mention of "mammon" is the only time I know when Jesus actually cites, by name, a competitor to the lordship of God.

No one can serve two masters. Either you will hate

the one and love the other, or you will be devoted

to the one and despise the other. You cannot serve
both God and money [mammon]. (Matt. 6:24)

Let me clarify, just in case you're tempted to accuse me of heresy.
I am not suggesting that money is a legitimate competitor to the
worship of God. Of course not. When we make money an idol, it
stops being a tool and instead becomes a godlike idol in our lives.
Slowly but surely, it seduces us and infiltrates our view of the world.
Like all other idols, money takes our focus away from the centrality
of Jesus in our lives.

So be wary of the love of money.

The worship of money.

The envy of money.

The lust for money.

The idolatry of money.

It's very clear to me that money and the global economy is what
drives this world. It also influences decisions that favor "the haves"
rather than the "have-nots."

Money influences many of the major decisions in the countries
where we live, filtering down to our communities, churches, and
neighborhoods. I believe that when we look at the whole picture, it's
rare for major decisions to favor the world's poorest. This is why we
must advocate for the poor. This is why, as followers of Jesus Christ,
we have to fight for the rights of the poor.

What I don't want to do, however, is to only make this about
how our governments deal with mammon. Money doesn't just
impact the decisions of others. It impacts my decisions. Your decisions. Every day.

How does money rule you? And what are you doing about it? What role do you believe simplicity has or can have in your life to weaken the power money has over you?

These are questions we should ask ourselves not only today but *every day*. So many of us want to serve Christ, but we want to serve Him on our terms. We want to ask people to move toward generosity without the personal commitment to live generously. I'm reminded of a man Jesus met, a man we know as the "rich young ruler." He was an upstanding, religious man who was trying to serve the Lord. He approached Jesus with a question for which he likely already had answers in mind:

> Just then a man came up to Jesus and asked, "Teacher, what good thing must I do to get eternal life?"
>
> "Why do you ask me about what is good?" Jesus replied. "There is only One who is good. If you want to enter life, keep the commandments."
>
> "Which ones?" he inquired.
>
> Jesus replied, "'You shall not murder, you shall not commit adultery, you shall not steal, you shall not give false testimony, honor your father and mother,' and 'love your neighbor as yourself.'"
>
> "All these I have kept," the young man said. "What do I still lack?"
>
> Jesus answered, "If you want to be perfect, go, sell your possessions and give to the poor, and you will have treasure in heaven. Then come, follow me."
>
> When the young man heard this, he went away sad, because he had great wealth. (Matt. 19:16–22)

Jesus ministered to the rich young ruler. Jesus pierced this young ruler's soul and knew that his greed held him captive. Jesus knew money (mammon) was the young ruler's idol, and this idol prevented him from growing in faith, trust, and discipleship.

Think about the rich young ruler for a moment.

Wealth. Youth. Power. Triple gold.

We have to ask ourselves a question here: Is it possible that Christ might be challenging us to live life with loose hands? I don't know about you, but I have a hard time seeing myself as the rich young ruler. I'm not rich, I'm no longer young, and I'm certainly not a ruler. And yet, I have all the comforts this young man enjoyed, and more. Perhaps, we are much more like the rich young ruler than we imagine. I can't help but be challenged by these words from Francis Bacon, the English philosopher: "Money is a good servant but a bad master."

We live in remarkable times, and we all have remarkable resources. I expect that most of the people reading this live more luxurious lives than this rich young ruler, who was considered rich in his day. We take so much for granted today. You probably have all the food you can eat, clean water, unlimited access to information, and unimaginable comforts. Yet we don't see ourselves as rich, because there is always someone richer.

Hello, Big Money

Congratulations! If you have the privilege to read this, you are likely one of (drumroll, please) the world's richest people! Holla! Raise the roof! Break out the Cristal!

No, seriously. I've got news for you. You. Are. Rich.

Really. No joke.

According to the website www.globalrichlist.com, with my annual income of $68,000 (when we birthed ODW) as a senior pastor of a church in Seattle, I am a member of the 1 percent club. To be more specific, I rank among the world's richest. I know you're familiar with folks such as Bill Gates, Warren Buffett, and Oprah, who often find themselves on the top of the world's richest people list.

But I am actually ranked too.

Specifically, as I write this, I am ranked 8,161,376th in the world. That means that my income puts me at the top 0.14 percent of wealth in the world, by dollars earned in a year. Here is an amazing fact: You need only an average salary in America to become part of the 1 percent of earners globally—where the annual average daily salary is $180.[2]

To consider what the injustice of global poverty looks like, let's first look at a few statistics:

- One in three human beings live on less than two dollars a day. That's 2.4 billion people.[3]
- One in five human beings live in extreme poverty, scraping by on just $1.25 a day. Imagine five quarters in the palm of your hand—your income to eat, pay for school, health expenses, and a place to live.[4]
- One in ten people alive today do not have safe water to drink. When they take a sip of water, it's probably tinted brown and filled with disease.[5]

- One in three people live without access to improved sanitation.[6]
- Every two minutes a woman dies due to complications during pregnancy or childbirth, likely with no medication, hospital, or birthing suite.[7]

The majority of the world lives with this kind of pain every day. Life for the men, women, and children in extreme poverty consists of trying to scrape by day to day, and often they fail to even do that. It's no wonder so many people in extreme poverty cannot grasp the idea of planning for tomorrow, when all they can focus on is satisfying the hungry rumble in their bellies today.

So not only are we blessed, but we are filthy rich in comparison to the larger world. If you live in the developed world, you have won the "DNA lottery,"[8] as Bono so eloquently sings, and are insanely rich compared to the vast majority of humans.

We are each the rich young ruler.

There must be a shift in our self-perception and our self-awareness. Maybe we're far closer to being the rich young ruler than we ever imagined.

Often we look only at faraway places ... at the distant ... across the ocean ... to see people living in extreme poverty. Poverty is also in our backyards, in our neighborhoods, and in our churches.

Census figures for the United States released in September 2012 reveal record-high numbers of Americans continue to live in poverty.

The latest data reveal:

One out of seven people in the USA are living in poverty.

- The Census Bureau reports that 46.2 million people were living in poverty in the United States in 2011—the largest number of persons counted as poor in the 53 years of poverty measurements.
- The poverty rate (the percentage of all people in the United States who were poor) also remained at record high levels [in 2011]: 15 percent for all Americans and 21.9 percent for children.

Almost one out of sixteen people in the USA are living in deep poverty.

- The Census defines people in deep poverty when they make 50% below the poverty line (family of four living on $23,050 a year); Census figures show that, in 2011, 6.6 percent of all people [in the USA], or 20.4 million people, lived in deep poverty.

Racial and ethnic minorities, the disabled, women, children, and families headed by single women are particularly vulnerable to poverty and deep poverty.

- In 2011, 9.8% of non-Hispanic whites (19.2 million) lived in poverty and 4.4% in deep poverty;

25.3% of Hispanics (13.2 million) lived in poverty and 10.5% in deep poverty; and 27.6% of
blacks (10.9 million) lived in poverty and 12.8%
in deep poverty.

- Although blacks represent 13.1% of the general
population, they represent 27.6% of the poor
population. Hispanics, who make up 16.7%
of the population, represent 25.3% of the poor
population.

- In 2011, more than 5 million more women than
men lived in poverty.

- 57.2% of children under age 6 living in poverty
are children of single mothers.[9]

It's clear by these figures that if we really want to serve the poor,
we need to look to those living among us. In fact, they are likely next
door.

The Lure of Upward Mobility Culture

You wouldn't know we have everything we need by observing popular
culture, or by flipping on the TV and watching a few commercials.
The average kid watches twenty thousand thirty-second TV commercials in a year.[10]

The message coming through is: "Life is insufficient. You are
insufficient. I am insufficient. You need more. I need more. We all
need more. And once we get more, we'll be happier ... until we need
more. Again."

And then the cycle continues. Sometimes we hear this in subtle ways, sometimes in not-so-subtle ways.

Once we have a lot, then we want more. We always lack something. So what is the antidote for this dangerous and seductive poison? What cures this endless drumbeat of commercialism, telling us that we are not adequate without a certain product?

Again, I'm reminded of the great power in the story of Jesus. There are so many things that compel me about Jesus, but one of them is what I call "the story of downward mobility." It completely contradicts the movement of upward mobility that is pervasive in our culture. We want to upgrade everything at every opportunity: We want the bestest, the fastest, the slickest, the coolest, the newest, the largest, the most horsepowerest, and the list goes on …

Even as I'm writing this book on my laptop, I want … I need … I lust … for the latest MacBook Pro with Retina display, ultrabook, superbook, miraclebook …

But I digress.

Upward mobility never stops, because we go through this cycle constantly.

The incarnation is the story of how Jesus humbled Himself and chose not to exercise His divine rights, instead choosing to take on flesh and bone and assume full humanity—being fully God but also fully man.

Born in a manger to simple commoners, Jesus assumed a simple lifestyle as a carpenter. Throughout His life, He owned nothing but the things He could take with Him. His life is the mind-boggling, heart-compelling, countercultural story of downward mobility.

This is a lesson and a story we all have to get behind. This is the Jesus we have to get behind—*the Jesus of downward mobility*. He is not the Jesus of bling-bling, the Jesus of total prosperity theology, a Jesus of exclusivity and elitism, a Jesus of health and wealth, or the Jesus of "send forty-nine dollars and we'll mail you this special anointed cloth for your personal miracle."

Now, I am not suggesting that we all adopt a lifestyle of absolute poverty but rather a theology, praxis, and *lifestyle of enough*.

We have enough.

We are blessed and blessed immensely.

God has given us enough.

God is our enough.

I'm reminded of the wise words G. K. Chesterton said: "There are two ways to get enough. One is to continue to accumulate more and more. The other is to desire less."[11]

A lesson for us all to consider: Upward mobility may "win," but downward mobility is countercultural. This is why people are so fascinated by a pastor and his family giving up his annual salary. This is why stories of people giving up their savings for people they don't know are remarkable. This is why people are fascinated by someone who gives up a "good life" to go abroad and serve the poor.

Contentment does not come from our upward mobility. Our contentment comes from a life of gratitude and generosity. Our contentment comes in living in the truth that Jesus emptied Himself and invites us to live in countercultural obedience to Him.

As much as it is expected or desired in our culture, there will never be a price tag on contentment.

I Hate Moving!

Probably like you, I hate moving. It always results in lots of work, sore muscles, and inevitably, it takes much longer than anticipated. One of the big reasons why I hate moving is that it challenges me about my junk. Now, this is more poignant if you understand that Minhee and I pride ourselves on "living simply." We often think we succeed in this endeavor … until we have to move. What happens then? We're often shocked by how much stuff we've accumulated. And I look at my wife and say, "Repent!" because I want to blame someone else for *my* own excess.

This was a real point of conviction when Minhee and I were preparing to launch One Day's Wages. We started digging into our stuff and realized how much we had accumulated over the years. When Minhee and I got married in 1997, she brought her two large bags of possessions and I had a guitar, several boxes of books, and a large bag of clothes. We didn't own a bed and thus slept on the wooden floor of our one-bedroom apartment. We didn't have a television or any other furniture, with the exception of a dining table. Fast-forward about fourteen years and, oh, how times have changed.

Well, during this time of self-examination and preparation for ODW, we identified many things to sell to reach our goal. Minhee found clothes to sell to secondhand stores. The kids hosted garage sales. And yes, as much as I wanted to, I could not ignore the Miata. That also went toward our goal of pledging one year's wages.

We chose for a season, besides basic necessities, not to buy anything. When we bought clothes, it was at Goodwill (hipster alert!).

We invited our kids into the discussion and purpose. They understood what they could comprehend at their respective ages and were also committed. This was a family endeavor, a family response to God's conviction on our hearts. We explained to them that for a season we would cut back on everything. It was inconvenient, difficult, and at times even painful. But it particularly challenged the false idea that we didn't have enough.

I will never forget the moments when I surveyed my garage—the garage in which I cannot presently park a vehicle—and wondered, *How is this living a life of simplicity? Where in the world did I get all this stuff?*

In his compelling and challenging book *Rich Christians in an Age of Hunger*, Dr. Ronald J. Sider wrote poignantly about the need for Christians (and all of us) to examine our lives but also to take action:

> We need to make some dramatic, concrete moves to escape the materialism that seeps into our minds via diabolically clever and incessant advertising. We have been brainwashed to believe that bigger houses, more prosperous businesses, and more sophisticated gadgets are the way to joy and fulfillment. As a result, we are caught in an absurd, materialistic spiral. The more we make, the more we think we need in order to live decently and respectably. Somehow we have to break this cycle because it makes us sin against our needy brothers and sisters and, therefore, against our Lord. And it also destroys us. Sharing with others is the way to real joy.[12]

If we disagree with the challenges of prophetic voices in our lives, perhaps we can listen to the wisdom and challenge of Jesus Himself, who said:

> Do not store up for yourselves treasures on earth, where moths and vermin destroy, and where thieves break in and steal. But store up for yourselves treasures in heaven, where moths and vermin do not destroy, and where thieves do not break in and steal. For where your treasure is, there your heart will be also. (Matt. 6:19–21)

Those words of wisdom remind me of a meeting my wife and I had with a friend in Korea in the summer of 2008. At the time, we were preparing to launch ODW. She's a European "foreigner" living in Korea as a missionary and a follower of Christ. She's learned the Korean language and after two decades has adopted the customs and cultures. She has grown to love the people of Korea and beyond. She and her husband have also adopted a lifestyle of simplicity.

This is different from a life of poverty. They've chosen to live as simply as possible—free from the stuff we often find ourselves *loving*, *lusting*, and *labeling*.

During our conversation, she shared her enthusiasm for our vision to fight global poverty and her commitment to keep us in prayer. That in itself was deeply edifying and encouraging. She proceeded to share that she didn't have any money to donate at that time, and we explained that her emotional and spiritual support meant a great deal.

What happened next … *we will never forget.*

She opened her shoulder bag and proceeded to take out seven small boxes and explained, "My husband and I have committed to live a life of simplicity, and we don't have money to support your vision. But I love and believe in what you guys are doing."

There was a pause as Minhee and I looked at each other, not quite sure where the conversation was going.

"These boxes contain my jewelry," she continued. "They are my heirlooms. I don't need them. I want to give them to your organization. Please sell them and use the proceeds to help the poorest of the poor."

Wow. We were so humbled. Shortly after that conversation, the Holy Spirit convicted me with these questions:

Where is your treasure?

Who is your treasure?

Destroy the Demon Greed

I once heard from a sociologist that a person in the Western world spends about 80 percent of his or her awake time engaged with money: earning it, spending it, or dreaming about it. So while money is a tool for us to use, if we're not careful, it's easy for the "love of money" to become a godlike, idolatrous force in our lives. Author and theologian Richard Foster wrote in his book *The Challenge of the Disciplined Life* that "giving frees us from the tyranny of money."[13]

Foster went on to say, "Just the very act of letting go of money, or some other treasure, does something within us. It destroys the demon greed."[14] And it has been said, "If you're enslaved by greed, you cannot lead."[15]

Foster said that if we don't learn how to control money, it will control us because it is so seductive. This marks the distinction between money and mammon. Money—when it controls us—is no longer a tool but instead becomes godlike and, thus, mammon in our lives. And so, we have to ask ourselves the question: Do we control money or does it control us?

"Jesus Christ and all the writers of the New Testament call us to break free of mammon lust and live in joyous trust," Foster says in his book *Freedom of Simplicity*. "They point us toward a way of living in which everything we have we receive as a gift, and everything we have is cared for by God, and everything we have is available to others when it is right and good. This reality frames the heart of Christian simplicity. It is the means of liberation and power to do what is right and to overcome the forces of fear and avarice."[16]

Instead of having those things rule us, we need to pursue and practice a theology of generosity, simplicity, and contentment.

The Wrath of Upward Mobility

Marketers, advertisers, and salespeople bank on us wanting more. They want us to buy into the idea of upward mobility. They know human beings fall into the out-of-control trap of consumerism. And so we spend beyond our means. I have always thought it was odd that my college information packet included numerous credit card applications. These ads had very few legible details, just fine print, but there were huge photos showing happy people, flush with cash. No interest for three months, they said. As if it were all free money.

A lot of things have changed since I went to college. For one thing the amount of debt is skyrocketing. An average member of the graduating class today leaves college with approximately $35,000 in debt, including $3,000 in credit card debt.[17]

One positive trend is the movement in the past few years to limit the marketing of credit cards on college campuses. Card companies are now prohibited from "offering students freebies, such as T-shirts or pizza, in exchange for signing up for a card on campus or at school events, and college groups are required to make public any partnerships they have with card issuers."[18]

Still, Americans of all ages are neck-deep in debt. Right now, Americans who use credit cards carry more than $5,000 in debt, on average.[19] That's per account. It's a tough figure to nail down, because there are many ways to measure it. But the point being—we have a lot of debt in this country.

And consider this: Almost 40 percent of households carry a balance month to month, averaging more than $7,000 in balance carryover. Those seeking credit counseling usually have $24,000 in debt, carrying about seven cards on average.[20]

We cannot ever quench this desire until we find a deeper satisfaction in life.

Flip the Paradigm

I recently heard a story about a woman named Dr. Eleanor Sutherland, a family physician in Federal Way, Washington, who passed away in

2012. She had lived very simply, and her lifestyle allowed her the flexibility in her time and finances to be extraordinarily generous. Her closest cohorts in serving others were her sister Kathleen and friend Beatrice.

Eleanor grew up extremely poor, so she elected to attend medical school in Germany because it was more affordable and more women were enrolled. A friend of Eleanor's and the trustee of her estate, Paul Birkey, said that Eleanor cared about health-care reform before it became a topic in popular culture. Her version of health-care reform was simple: She charged a fraction of the going rate and did not turn anyone away because he or she couldn't pay.

Paul wrote in an obituary:

> Eleanor's boundless passion for medicine, as with her boundless passion for everything, was fueled by and undergirded with her passion to serve God and Jesus Christ. In every way, she led life as a mission with Christ's teachings as her template and guide. Her medical practice, her travels abroad, her everyday life and her supreme self-confidence all were guided by her all encompassing faith....
>
> Nothing was wasted—if a patient needed a wheelchair, walker or cane, she would round one up, probably a well used one. She wheedled pharmaceutical reps for samples she could give away. Perhaps most importantly, each and every patient was listened to carefully and treated in the

context of their lives, as a whole person. Her sense of humor was not the ordinary kind; it was an insightful, eloquent, smart alecky kind—always kind and always present.[21]

Paul said that if you knew Eleanor, you had probably been chided for not being sufficiently thrifty. She saved wrapping paper, sat in the dark to save candles, and wore used clothing. She wanted to put herself last so that she would be able to give as Christ taught us to give: generously and unconditionally.

At age eighty-five, Eleanor died at home, as she wanted. She left a small fortune to charities and a legacy of compassion to her friends and clients.

She had the supernatural vision to see that her money was not her own, but instead was for God's kingdom.

Rest in peace, Eleanor.

Our works and actions do not save us, but they do proclaim and bear witness to our faith.

Enjoy Your Philanthropy, Millionaire

Your generosity does not have to be *just* a transactional experience. We can experience so much more joy and spiritual impact with our philanthropy.

From time to time Minhee and I try to step back from our giving, look at the big picture, and then develop a strategy about how and why we give. We experienced a big shift a few years ago in the way we saw our finances. When I realized that 80 percent of the world lives on less than ten US dollars a day, it prompted a shift in how we saw our roles in the larger world.

As a single-income family (back when we started ODW) living in Seattle, we were just trying to get by. It felt laborious at times because Seattle is an expensive city. We had the usual expenses, such as our mortgage, car payments, and bills. We also have three kids. They like to eat. *Like every day.* Like five times a day.

Sooner or later, you get into the mind-set that you do not have enough. You start comparing yourself with others. For example, I get stressed and insecure when I hear of other parents saving up for their kids' 529s and their IRAs, and other technical financial terms that I'm still not entirely sure I understand.

One paradigm shift helped me take a step back and see the big picture of my finances: I added up my salary over forty years. In doing so, I realized that *I am a millionaire.*

At an annual salary of $68,000, and not factoring in salary increases, I would be earning about $2.7 million over that forty-year span. That's a lot of money. I know there are day-to-day, month-to-month expenses, tithing, taxes, and many other commitments, but it was so helpful for me to get a big-picture perspective, and thus, a grander vision of how I can live generously.

I'm not suggesting that you have to replicate what our family chose to do in giving an entire year's wages to a cause. That was simply our response to a personal conviction. However, I would encourage you to pray and ask God to move you to live a life of generosity.

Shift your heart and mind as it concerns stewardship. Rather than thinking, *What of my stuff should I give back to God?* I invite you to think, *Everything I own belongs to God.*

The Most Beautiful Donation

As the founder of One Day's Wages, I've seen my share of donations come in all shapes, sizes, and amounts. I've also witnessed beautiful campaigns as people have donated their birthdays for a cause, run marathons to raise funds, or even cycled across America. We've had our share of $1 donations (everything helps!) and the occasional $10,000 donation as well.

There's one donation that stands out to me. I often refer to it as "the most beautiful donation" we've received at One Day's Wages. In fact, I remember the exact day because I was sitting in front of my computer screen when I read the note that accompanied the donation.

It was September 25, 2012.

This wasn't a huge donation. Far from it. In fact, it was a donation in the amount of $73, but with the donation came this accompanying note: *How about an eight-hour shift at Subway?*

A sixteen-year-old boy named Tyler worked a day's shift and donated his day's wages for ODW's education fund.

Tears came to my eyes because it perfectly captured the heart of what I believe about philanthropy, generosity, and about the vision of One Day's Wages.

Philanthropy and generosity are not reserved for the elite. You don't have to be a rock star, a millionaire, or a celebrity to be generous. The root word of *philanthropy* literally means "love of humanity," and this is something we can all do. This is something we must all do. This kind of love can change the world. And when we live this simple truth, we'll be changed ourselves.

Thank you, Tyler.

Everything I Needed Was Right in Front of Me

Sometimes we look at being blessed only from a financial perspective. That's why I think it was so jarring and so good for us to realize that while we had lost so much, we still had enough. In fact, we had more than enough. I had to let go of the car and the home where we lived (for a time), and we couch surfed. Our bank account was nearly empty.

When Minhee and I told our kids we were going to move out of our house for a time, to raise $10,000, it was difficult beyond words—far more difficult than I had imagined.

However, several weeks after moving into a friend's extra bedroom, our family was just hanging out in the room; our blankets and sleeping bags lay on the floor. For a while, we all did our own things, including reading, surfing on our gadget devices, and napping, but eventually, we all turned our focus and attention to a family game of Scrabble.

After several weeks the initial pain, shame, and self-pity had eased, and we were all getting used to our current reality. That day, we laughed, smiled, and enjoyed ourselves as we played Scrabble.

And then I had a moment. An epiphany. I sensed the whisper of God speaking gently into my spirit.

"Eugene, look and see. Open your eyes. See how I have lavished My gifts upon you! See how I have blessed you!"

I had placed so much of my value and worth in material stuff and my ability to provide those things for my family. But everything I truly needed was right in front of me. The greatest treasures and blessings:

Our faith and hope in Christ.

My marriage and love for Minhee.

Our children: Jubilee, Trinity, and Jedi.

Our church community.

B – L – E – S – S – E – D.

I don't know how many points that wins you in Scrabble, but all I know is that it is the T– R – U – T – H.

Chapter 4

SHUT UP, LISTEN, AND PRAY

Sh. Take a moment here.

Let's be honest. We live in a busy world, with busy lives and busy schedules.

Busy, busy, busy.

Go, go, go.

Busy, busy, busy.

Go, go, go.

Repeat.

Sound familiar? It sure does to me. In a culture that elevates busyness and quick action as badges of leadership and faith, this may be one of the most critical chapters for some of you. With so much noise and chaos in our busy lives, we need to create space to listen to God's voice. We need to let solitude and silence be our allies, not our enemies. The process of introspection in writing this chapter has been the most convicting part of this book for me.

Blah, Blah, Blah

We live in a world inundated with noise. We consume ourselves with media in various forms: television, radio, talk shows, music, the Internet, smartphones, tablets, laptops, desktops, and more.

The average American over the age of two watches about five hours and eleven minutes of television every day.[1] That translates into about thirty-six hours of television every week. This means that an average American will spend nine years glued to the television over a life span.

9 years.

108 months.

3,285 days.

78,840 hours.

4,730,400 minutes.

Let these numbers sink in for a moment.

Now consider these statistics that convey the absolute inundation of all forms of media in our society:

- The percentage of households that have at least one television is 99 percent, and in fact, the average TV household owns 2¼ TV sets.
- The percentage of US homes that own three or more TV sets is 66 percent. Wow, that's a lot of TVs.
- The percentage of Americans who regularly watch television while eating dinner is 66 percent.

- Parents spend an average of about 3.5 minutes a week in meaningful conversation with their children.
- An average child spends 1,680 minutes (that's 28 hours per week) watching television.[2]

Consider the fast-changing frontier of the Internet and new media. New media is changing so rapidly that various research sources can't even agree how much time the average person spends online—on desktops, smartphones, and tablets—and oftentimes, we're surfing multiple devices at the same time.

We're living in extraordinary times with extraordinary resources but are simultaneously inundated with so much clutter, noise, and static. In a world where we are constantly bombarded in this way, *sometimes we just need to shut up, listen, and pray.*

Mother Teresa is almost universally loved and respected for her compassion and care for the poor through an organization she founded called Missionaries of Charity. The importance of prayer and silence in her life was often overshadowed by her loving and caring for orphans, the poor, the abandoned, and the sick. With so much burden, expectation, and need, it was the discipline of prayer and silence that gave her vision and perspective. She once said, "Silence gives us a new outlook on everything. We need silence to be able to touch souls."[3]

With so much noise and the ever-present temptation to go, move, act, and do something, how important is it for us to wait and listen to God? How important is it as we seek to do the work of God? Richard Foster articulates this point: "In prayer we wait in the power of God for the evil to dissipate and the good to rise up.... Through prayer we develop the longing, the yearning to sink down deep into the things of God."[4]

With the clutter of so much noise and the temptation to place ourselves in the center of everything and engage in self-reliance, prayer helps us to "sink down deep" in the heart, work, ways, and kingdom of God.

Gary Haugen, the founder of International Justice Mission and author of *Just Courage,* wrote:

> Mother Teresa said that she couldn't imagine doing her work for more than thirty minutes without prayer. Do you and I have work that we can't imagine doing for thirty minutes without prayer?...
>
> I won't need to be in prayer every thirty minutes in my work if I don't really need God's power to get it done, or if it's work that God doesn't really need done because it has nothing to do with his kingdom.
>
> At IJM, we begin every working day with thirty minutes of silence and prayerful preparation for the day, and then we all gather again for prayer at 11 a.m. We don't do this so much as a matter of discipline but out of desperation. We don't think we can do the mission God has called us to or love each other the way we ought to without spiritual resources accessed through prayer.[5]

I love the witness and wisdom of Mother Teresa, especially when she highlights the importance of prayer and silence—but the truth is that we don't need her to prove that they are important. If we read the Scriptures and focus on the life of a guy named Jesus, then it's clear how important prayer and silence were to Him as a regular spiritual rhythm. Jesus stayed busy with teaching, meetings, mentoring, leadership training, rebuking, healing, exorcising, resurrecting, feeding thousands, and walking on water.

Everyone wanted a piece of Him. But look at what Jesus did. Even before He engaged in public ministry, He retreated to the desert for prayer, fasting, and solitude (see Matt. 4:1–11). Then throughout His ministry, Jesus intentionally took time to rest, retreat, pray, and honor the Sabbath:

At daybreak, Jesus went out to a solitary place. (Luke 4:42)

Very early in the morning, while it was still dark, Jesus got up, left the house and went off to a solitary place, where he prayed. (Mark 1:35)

Jesus went out to a mountainside to pray, and spent the night praying to God. (Luke 6:12)

After he had dismissed them, he went up on a mountainside by himself to pray. Later that night, he was there alone. (Matt. 14:23)

If Jesus—the Son of God, our Messiah and Savior, fully God and fully man, perfect God and perfect man—needed to retreat for rest, solitude, and prayer, how much more do we as mere women and men need to engage in these gifts and disciplines regularly?

I'll say it again: Shut up, listen, and pray.

And keep doing it. Build a rhythm.

Change the World in Three Easy Steps

I'd love to make my dreams happen with just a snap of my fingers. Wouldn't you?

Snap. I'd love to have access to a functioning "easy button." I'd love to have the secret formula to world change in three simple steps.

Despite my best efforts to carry out my plans in such simplistic and pain-free ways, it is rarely quick and easy. The truth is that every significant plan, event, or project I've tackled has taken longer to carry out than I originally planned. The event or project has almost always been delayed. Translation? My plans and timing versus God's plans and timing are often different.

Enduring a delay has often been a blessing in disguise. Although it doesn't seem that way when I go through the process of waiting, laboring, waiting, praying, waiting, and working, when I look back in nearly every situation, these times of growth are expressions of God's grace.

I should remember this the next time I try to push forward my agenda in haste.

Being forced to shut up, listen, and pray—only to be met by God's very presence—is truly God's grace.

Our Quest for an Urban, Multiethnic Church

Right after seminary at Princeton, I got a job at a predominantly Korean church in the suburbs of northern Seattle. I'd been working there as a pastor for three years when I felt a strong calling to plant a church in the city of Seattle.

Our dream was to plant and grow an urban, multiethnic church. We wanted to seek Jesus in every way, living out the Micah 6:8 call "to act justly and to love mercy and to walk humbly with [our] God." With blessings from our church in the suburbs, we embarked on this journey.

Minhee and I were anxious but excited. As I often do, I developed a plan, created a timeline, devised a strategy, and wrote a manifesto. I felt a clear call by God to start this urban church that we called Quest. I had outlined everything in a "one, two, three—bam, bam, bam!" strategy. Instead of everything happening quickly, our "bam, bam, bam!" became more of a "slam, slam, slam!"

Minhee and I faced closed door after closed door. Needless to say, this long process was frustrating and discouraging.

A couple of months after we left our previous church, Minhee and I faced reality: Our church plant was not going to happen in the time frame we'd expected. Those people who'd expressed or committed financial resources to our church plant were impacted by the dot-com implosion of 2000 and were no longer able to help. Folks who were interested in being part of our launch team were no longer interested, willing, or able—for various reasons. My strategies, manifesto, and plans for launching a church were simply not working out.

Also, at this point in our marriage, we had another growing concern. We already had one little girl, and another baby was on the way.

This was a humbling time. We had to face certain realities in our life. We had bills and obligations. To be blunt, I needed a job. *Any job.*

Will preach for food.

Taco Bell Rejected Me

When I speak to students at seminaries, I joke and tell them, "Be careful. Your degree in seminary will soon make you useless to society."

Yes, I always strive to inspire.

Even though I had advanced degrees, or perhaps because of that, I ran into many dead ends as I looked for work. Seriously, no one knows what a master of divinity degree is. No one. The *magister divinitatis.*

I discovered after several frustrating months of job searching that just listing a master of divinity on your résumé can be confusing, unless you are applying for a position at a church.

"An MDiv?" they ask.

How about an *M-Don't?*

People would look at my résumé and say, "You're overqualified." Or they were just mystified. Or they were suspicious because I was a pastor, wondering if something bad or scandalous had happened forcing me out of ministry. Or perhaps I was a religious nut who wanted to convert all their workers to my personal Cho cult.

I rewrote my résumé accordingly, as the bills kept coming, and I kept searching everywhere. I was applying at fast-food restaurants and retail. Anything. Starbucks. Wendy's. One of the low points was going into Toys "R" Us, where they had a huge banner that advertised, "Hiring for Christmas!" I thought, *How can I possibly not land this job during the holiday season?*

Even that didn't happen. Fail.

Then there was Taco Bell. I thought I had a good chance at Taco Bell. I was a customer, and I was sure I could assemble a Nachos Bellgrande, because I've eaten many of them. So I filled out a job application and spoke with the manager.

"Great. We'll check your references and will get back to you at some point."

"Awesome. Thank you. Looking forward to hearing from you."

But, no, I never heard back. I'd been turned down by Taco Bell.

Reality check: I searched for work everywhere. The economy got worse, and I was growing increasingly discouraged. I had a family to support. Minhee's belly was only getting bigger, which is what happens when someone is pregnant, and before we knew it, she was due to give birth any day.

The Lord Provides

I had been looking for work for about six months, and though we had been praying and sensed that God wanted us to plant a church, I was beginning to have my doubts. In fact, I had doubts about everything. I felt sorry for myself and asked lots of questions. I had no job, no income, no church to return to, and no church to start—I was utterly discouraged.

Discouragement soon became frustration and bitterness. Eventually, I just became angry with God and everything.

I remember one night in particular. Minhee was nearly full-term in her pregnancy. For you folks out there who don't know what that means, it means "she could give birth at any moment." We didn't know how we were going to pay for the birth. I remember assisting Minhee to bed because of her back, and then I went into my office.

That night, I just snapped. I lost control.

It was during this time in my office that I prayed, and in prayer, I realized that I hadn't prayed for months. I'm not talking about the prayers before meals or the prayers I routinely prayed with my baby daughter, Jubilee, before I tucked her into bed.

I'm talking about the kind of prayers for which we create time to seek out the God of the universe. We seek the God who knows us, loves us, saves us, and calls us. These are the prayers of raw honesty and intense listening, the prayers of desperation, the prayers of humility and confession.

That night, I prayed.

In my honesty, my prayers oozed intensity, and even bitterness, confusion, and anger. In the midst of many tears streaming down my face, I remember these words venting from my lips:

> God, I am so upset at You.
> I am so hurt. I am so angry about what is happening.
> Nothing is going as I planned.
> I feel like I've lost control of my life.

In that moment I heard God. I heard the Holy Spirit speaking to me. Literally. I wish I could tell you that I regularly hear the voice of God, but that simply wouldn't be true. Only on two occasions have

I felt as though I've heard God literally speaking to me, and this was one of those occasions. What did I hear?

These words:

Finally. Finally you understand.
You don't have control over your life.
Surrender to Me, Eugene.

His words hit me. And they were righteous and convicting. I wept even more.

Even in this pain, I rejoiced because I had felt God was so far away, so distant, or so occupied with other things in the larger cosmos. But even in this rebuke, I sensed His intimate presence and accepted His love. I may have felt the boat was capsizing and I was drowning, but all along, God was near and calling me to trust and surrender.

Two days later, Minhee and I went to the hospital for a weekly checkup with her doctor, but on that appointment, Dr. Wells thought it would be best for Minhee to be given a room at the Evergreen hospital. After Minhee checked in, took a bath, and lay on the bed, she began having birth pains. She screamed a couple of words I can't include in this book.

After the nurse came in to see what was going on, everything escalated, and then it all happened so quickly. The nurse and I saw the baby crown, and the nurse quickly summoned the doctor. Before the doctor arrived, and in less than five minutes, the nurse and I helped welcome our second child into the world. Literally.

Minhee and I named her Trinity. And it was glorious. We cried like babies. Including Trinity.

In her birth, we once again sensed God's amazing love and grace for us, and a reminder of His promises: *Surrender. Trust Me. I love you.*

Time Alone with God

The day after Trinity was born, Minhee was still at the hospital resting and we were eager to return home. In between visits to the hospital and our home, I made a quick visit to a local Barnes and Noble, the large retail bookstore, in search of a photo album for our new baby.

As I was coming out of the restroom, I ran into John, a congregant from my former church. To be honest, I was a bit embarrassed because he asked me how I was doing and, in particular, how the new church plant was doing.

I smiled, awkwardly dancing around the reality.

"Are you doing okay, Pastor Eugene?" John said.

"Yeah. Yeah … Actually, it's been a roller coaster. Minhee and I just welcomed our second child yesterday. We're thrilled, but we've been having a hard time starting the church. Actually, there is no church as of yet. I've actually been looking for a job for the past six months. Keep us in your prayers."

"Wow, Pastor Eugene. Congratulations on the baby, and I'm sorry to hear that it's been so difficult with church and job hunting."

"Yeah," I said as I began to retreat. "It's cool. Great seeing you."

"Actually, Pastor Eugene, wait a minute. If you want it, I can give you a job right now."

"What? Really? What job?"

"I'm here at Barnes and Noble today to sign a contract. I run a custodial services company, and I just landed a contract to provide services here. Um, do you want the job?"

"Wow. Okay. Sure. Yes."

And just like that, I began my new job as a custodian two days later. I could not help but chuckle as I was cleaning the toilet I had been sitting on two days before (I know, too much information).

After the first couple of days of excitement from just having a job, reality set in. I thought, *Wow. I'm a custodian.* It's not that there's anything wrong with being a custodian. Nothing at all. It's just that this was the furthest thing I had envisioned when I left my previous church job to plant Quest Church. It wasn't part of my strategic plan.

Furthermore, I quickly learned that it was incredibly difficult work. I had to clean a forty-thousand-square-foot store, by myself, in the early morning hours between six and nine. There was no time to fool around, so I had to set up a strategy: bathrooms, vacuuming, and then dusting. That was the game plan every day. When I arrived in the mornings, it was just me and the employees preparing to open the store. I went straight to the janitor's closet. I gathered my supplies and started working. I first headed to the bathrooms because they needed time to dry out. I scrubbed the toilets, cleaned the urinals and then the sinks, wiped the walls, restocked supplies, and finally mopped the floors.

And let me just say ... the women's bathrooms. Wow. Seriously, ladies. All this time I thought men's bathrooms were bad. Yikes! (Yes, I guess I am judging you!)

After cleaning the bathrooms, I quickly vacuumed. I needed to vacuum before the store opened at nine, so as not to disturb the customers. Dusting could continue once the doors opened.

I worked as fast as I possibly could. I sweated hard every day because there was rarely a moment to pause. It was all constant movement. For those three hours each morning, I experienced one of the hardest jobs I've ever had.

On top of that, the job was humbling and not what I had envisioned as my postseminary profession. If I'm honest, I struggled with my pride. My self-esteem. How I looked at myself. I had difficulties sharing with my family what was going on. I was always trying to hide how I was feeling. My responses were often, "I'm doing okay. Hanging in there."

That time in my life, and in the life of my family, was difficult and one of the most trying seasons of our lives. However, God surprised me by providing the Barnes and Noble janitorial job. He surprised me with His grace and developed my character in the face of these challenges. I worked hard and was able to provide for our family. The Lord gave us enough.

This was indeed an answer to prayer. After six months of looking for every kind of work, I could finally provide for my family. As a husband and a father, perhaps I place more emphasis on these things than I should. But it is important to me to take care of my wife, to take care of my kids. You see, during those months, Minhee and our kids were on a form of government-subsidized food stamp program—Women, Infants, and Children (WIC).

These humbling times also brought us moments of surprising grace and insight. For example, this season brought me to the WIC offices. To be honest, I didn't know what WIC was, and I had no relationship with anyone who was on the WIC program, or any other forms of food stamps.

In my previous years of being a pastor at a suburban church, topics of food stamps, WIC, or the poor never came up. So the first few times I had to go to the WIC office, I sat and waited (in trepidation) with immigrants, low-income families, and other human beings.

But what do I remember?

I remember that several people reached out to me, spoke to me, and asked about my story. Some, after hearing my story of being a pastor trying to plant a church, were so kind to pray for us. They ministered to me. God showed up in that place.

During that time we also learned, through the Washington State Department of Social and Health Services (DSHS) program for low-income families, that all expenses associated with Trinity's birth were retroactively covered by the state. The bills, complicated by a surgery Minhee required after giving birth, were absolutely enormous. We never could have afforded the cost. Then, just like that, 100 percent of our hospital bills were covered. Every single penny. Amazing. It was truly an answer to prayer.

This season wasn't just about a job or just about paying bills.

It was about us learning to surrender and to trust God.

It was about learning to be still before the Lord and seeking His voice and presence in our lives. My janitorial job lasted almost a year, but when I look back, it wasn't merely God providing for our family. It was also the process by which He resurrected the dry bones of my life amid the scarcity of faith and trust, and the clutter of so much noise and self-doubt. It was the journey by which God reignited my joy in, and reliance on, prayer.

I prayed in the most honest way I had in a long time. This is the challenge for professional clergy. Perhaps it is unfair for me to speak on behalf of all clergy, so let me just speak for myself. Prayer was, and is, a challenge for me. Praying in front of people can seductively become like a job. When you are a minister or a pastor, you pray because that's what you're supposed to do. Perhaps prayer is the challenge for you too. Perhaps it is the challenge for all of us.

At six o'clock in the morning, in a big, empty store, you're dusting, scrubbing, and vacuuming. When you do this kind of work for several hours, you're essentially all alone. No one watches you. There is no microphone or sound system. No video cameras. No one's tweeting or updating their Facebook status about how much they love your teaching or illustrations. There are no expectations (beyond clean bathrooms and floors). There is no liturgy to read or lead.

What do you do?

What can you do?

Well … *you pray.*

At least that's what I was compelled to do.

I had honest and raw conversations with God—a sequel of sorts to the prayer time that began in my office several weeks before I got the job. The prayers in these early mornings were so terrifying, refreshing, and convicting. It was just me and God talking, beyond the religious jargon, beyond the phrases, beyond the Christianese that we sometimes hide behind. God and me. Listening. Talking. Singing. Praying. Wrestling.

There were prayers of confession about self-reliance. About bitterness. About my schedule, my timetable (aka my Excel spreadsheet plans), my agenda, my dreams, and my will. The confession of the challenge of "my will be done versus Thy will be done."

As I hustled and sweated around that store, I prayed for Minhee, Jubilee, and Trinity, who was only weeks old. I prayed about the vision to plant a church. About wanting to listen to God well. Praying that God would bless this church. But again, being mindful about listening well and resisting my natural tendency to go before God. One of the best things that happened in that season of my life was that God used it to break me, to help me see and surrender to His will. I was reminded of these words from Henri Nouwen, one of my favorite writers: "Just as bread needs to be broken in order to be given, so, too, do our lives."[6]

As I sought clarity, answers, strategies, His favor, and divine appointments, God simply prompted me to ask myself, *To whom should I surrender?* I love the wisdom in this quote from C. S. Lewis that captures this truth: "I know now, Lord, why you utter no answer. You are yourself the answer."[7]

We can go through times that seem like spiritual and emotional deserts. In the barren landscape of those uncertain times, there's often a prime opportunity to pause. There's prime opportunity to pray and to listen for the voice of God speaking comfort and assurance through uncertainty.

We need to allow God to break us. We need to escape our self-absorbed blindness and see life illuminated in the light of God.

In other words, let's not be so consumed by our own visions that we forget the God who gave us those visions and dreams in the first place. We worship God, not our visions and dreams. We worship God, not our plans and strategies. Heed these beautiful words:

> Let us run with perseverance the race marked out
> for us, fixing our eyes on Jesus, the pioneer and per-
> fecter of faith. For the joy set before him he endured
> the cross, scorning its shame, and sat down at the
> right hand of the throne of God. (Heb. 12:1–2)

Indeed. May we fix our eyes on Jesus.

Seeing with Fresh Eyes

So if we do open our eyes, where do we look? With so many needs in the world, how can Christians know where and how to focus their efforts? We want to act.

As Christians, we have to be committed to the gospel, for its power is the essence of our faith. And by gospel, I am not speaking of some nebulous and abstract theological equation. I'm speaking of the story of God who created the universe, the world, and all that is good within it. I'm speaking of a God who sent His Son, Christ, to come to this world and to live among us.

I'm speaking of Jesus.

If you truly believe in the gospel, then you have to believe that it matters not just for your personal salvation and blessings but also for God's pursuit of restoration, redemption, and reconciliation for the entire world.

I believe in this gospel.

I live for this gospel.

I live for a gospel that not only saves but also serves; a gospel that not only saves but seeks to restore all things back unto the One that ushered forth all that is good and beautiful; a gospel that not only saves but ushers in the kingdom of God; a gospel that not only saves but restores the dignity of human beauty—even in the midst of our brokenness and depravity.

This gospel is not just for us. It is good news for all—especially for the least, the marginalized, the poor, the forgotten, the forsaken, and the alone. How can we not believe in this kind of gospel, when this gospel was first extended to us?

Truly, the gospel saves, but thankfully it does more than just save. The gospel not only saves, but it invites us to the life that God intended for us.

The gospel is not just the Four Spiritual Laws. It's not just our ticket to heaven. I'm not trying to diminish the importance of salvation, but to limit the depth and power of the gospel merely to salvation is simply a disservice to the gospel of Jesus Christ.

The gospel is also about a commitment to the kingdom of God, a kingdom that was ushered in by the incarnation and ministry of Jesus, the Christ.

If we believe in this kingdom and the gospel of Christ, we believe that Christ came, Christ died, Christ was raised, and Christ will return. The power of the Holy Spirit is at work all around us, so that we don't have to wait aimlessly until that day. I believe a sincere discipleship demonstrates itself by being active in the world today, because of Christ's example, and out of gratitude for God for everything we've been given.

As Christians, we should be about the work of God, the work of shalom, restoration, and redemption—in all the simplicity and profundity that this work requires.

We should be about the marathon and not about the sprint. We should not be defined by instant gratification. We should not be controlled by the mass broadcasting or the constant desire to communicate.

We live in a deeply narcissistic world. Narcissism is even more tempting today because of all the tools of social media. I mean, today we can't have lunch without telling people what we're eating or taking pictures of our food. C'mon, people. Stop taking photos of your food. Stop Instagramming … *Just eat your food.* Enjoy it. (This is a personal note to self.) I think we just have to realize that we live in a world in which narcissism is a struggle for many of us.

Before we're so quick to act and move and Instagram our food, may we …

Pray, discern, listen.

Pray, discern, listen.

Pray, discern, listen.

I would love for us to take more time to listen, pray, and allow God to speak, mold, and even break us.

Rebuild This City

I resonate with Nehemiah. I like him. I like the fact that he's a simple person with a simple job. He was a cupbearer—the guy who tasted the food and wine for the king to ensure that it wasn't poisoned. This was not necessarily the world's best job, especially if the food was poisoned. Nehemiah experienced hardships and struggles, including the experience of living in an exilic community. Nehemiah had no formal education: no big degrees, no fancy titles, and no experience with project management. Nehemiah was not the person you'd hire for an open position in your company, nonprofit, or church.

Nevertheless, there's much to appreciate in Nehemiah, and learn from him. He was a man who was not afraid to stop and truly listen for God's voice. And because of Nehemiah's willingness to listen to God and wait on Him, the Lord put on his heart an important and seemingly impossible vision.

In 721 BC, Assyria attacked Jerusalem. The city of God's chosen people was in bad shape, with the temple destroyed and the walls around the city in ruins.

As we've seen and experienced in our own lives, God allows suffering to take place. In the midst of this suffering, the people of Jerusalem forgot God, and they began to rebel against His ways. In spite of His people's rebellion and departure from relationship, God communicated His love for His people and an invitation to return to relationship. It didn't necessarily make the struggle any less difficult. God's chosen people were hurting.

During this time, Nehemiah felt convicted to rebuild the walls of Jerusalem. With that belief to rebuild came a secondary conviction to listen and pray. It was not an afterthought.

Here's what is absolutely astounding to me: After the Holy Spirit prompted Nehemiah's heart for this mission, scholars believe that his time of praying, confession, and repentance was not just a couple of days, but in actuality, they believe he engaged in this time for approximately four to six months.

In our time and context, four to six months may seem like an eternity. In this time, Nehemiah prays. He confesses. He repents. He listens. *He waits.*

This time humbles him, opens his eyes, breaks his heart, and gives him renewed vision:

> Then I said:
>
> "LORD, the God of heaven, the great and awesome God, who keeps his covenant of love with those who love him and keep his commandments, let your ear be attentive and your eyes open to hear the prayer your servant is praying before you day and night for your servants, the people of Israel. I confess the sins we Israelites, including myself and my father's family, have committed against you." (Neh. 1:5–6)

Nehemiah faced great opposition. He was tempted by power and position, and was threatened, bullied, agitated, and intimidated by a slew of adversaries led by Sanballat and Tobiah, and yet he remained steadfast through it all. He remained committed to the vision, and most important, he remained committed to God.

He took the time to pray before he embarked on this formidable task, and he took time during the process. This wasn't a quick decision. His vision shaped who he was, whom he served, and why.

Nehemiah was also not satisfied with a onetime prayer event, fasting, and listening and waiting. This wasn't just a show, an event, a conference, a gathering, or a public broadcast. For Nehemiah, this was an ongoing series of acts of submission, trust, and desperation as he prayed to God. Continuously doing these things simply became his identity as a servant of God. He knew that his actions would not be righteous if the motivation came from his own mind. Instead he wanted his actions and motivations coming from the heart of God.

The Act-Quick Culture

Deposit this word into your heart and mind: *Wait.*

Wait for the Lord …

Let's be honest—waiting may be one of the most difficult things for many of us. We live in an instant, fast-food, immediate-gratification culture. We do not want to wait. We hate lines. We want things … *now.*

So much of our culture, products, and consumer behavior hinges on getting what we want faster. Seconds count when it comes to how long it takes our computers to start. We cannot wait the extra thirty-four seconds.

When I'm waiting at the grocery store and have four items, I get upset because the person ahead of me has thirteen items.

This is actual dialogue I've played out in my mind: *Come on, lady. The sign says twelve items.* Twelve. *Not thirteen.* Then I begin to feel indignant, thinking, *This isn't fair and just! I must challenge this!*

I quietly mutter, "Twelve items … Twelve …"

I know because I count. I'm like the grocery-store Pharisee who counts twelve items. Okay, now I sound a little crazy.

The point is that we have such a hard time waiting. More than ever, we struggle with just being still. Our world and our hearts are flooded with information and the possibility for quick results and instant gratification.

Let's remind ourselves again: We should be about the marathon and not about the instant gratification. We don't need one-hit wonders—we need steady, faithful, and tenacious engagement in our discipleship.

Chronos

Hear this well: God's concept of time—*chronos* in ancient Greek—is much different from our concept of time, which is often defined as "now." We pray to God, and overnight we want an answer to that prayer. We expect responses from God immediately, because that's what we expect in every other aspect of our lives today.

If the answer isn't given to us in the way and time that we want, we say, "God, why have You forsaken me?"

God convicted Nehemiah to act justly, have faith, and invest his life in a mission much larger than he could imagine on his own. He was encouraged by circumstances to wait. And he had the wisdom to wait.

Let me be clear here. When I say to wait, I'm not equating the discipline of waiting to laziness or apathy. In his waiting, Nehemiah remained faithful. There is a difference between apathetic waiting and active, faith-drenched waiting. This kind of God-anticipating waiting encourages us. It compels us to pray, fast, seek discernment, and seek counsel.

Nehemiah did this not just for a day or for a conference or for a weekend retreat. Nehemiah engaged in this time of fasting, praying, and listening for at least four months and possibly up to six months. Nehemiah began this time of prayer in the Hebrew month of Nisan (Neh. 2:1), which is equivalent to March or April in our calendar. He prays continuously through the month of Kislev, which corresponds to the month of November or December. Nehemiah is an example of one who persevered in prayer. I call this the "waiting room." In our spiritual lives we have too many "drive-through windows" and not enough waiting rooms. While it's true that there are some who struggle with the lack of courage to pursue their dreams and convictions, the opposite is true as well. Many of us struggle with the temptation to act without listening, waiting, and using our God-given discernment.

When God gives us a vision, conviction, or dream, He may not want us to act upon it instantaneously. Instead, allow it to incubate in the waiting room. Some of us see the waiting room as weakness, but I believe it is an example of character and maturity.

Consider some of the significant characters in the Bible. Recall all the broken and flawed women and men whom God chose to use for His purposes and glory. Many of them learned the discipline of waiting and listening before responding to God's call.

Joseph waited thirteen years.

Abraham waited twenty-five years.

Moses waited forty years.

Rahab waited forty years.

Some speculate that Noah waited more than one hundred years to complete the building of the ark. Joseph waited in prison. Job waited in mourning. And Paul waited and waited for an answer for his prayer that God remove his thorn in the flesh.

Even Jesus waited thirty years to begin His ministry, and then He waited another forty days in the desert.

Emotion Versus Dedication and Prayer

I cannot tell you the number of conversations I've had with individuals who share thoughts, ideas, convictions, and passions that
eventually seem to fizzle out. Some of these passions last only a few
days or weeks. This repeating narrative I hear and see is one of the
primary reasons I was inspired to write this book.

More often than I can count, people come to me with an idea
and tell me they are inspired to do something. A passion. An initiative. A nonprofit. A ministry. A new "game changer."

This is what I tell them: "That's great! I'm so excited for you.
Come back in six months. Let me know if you're still convinced
this is a God-breathed dream in your life. Let me know if you still
feel compelled to pursue this, after giving it time. Pray and fast.
Come back to me six months from now, and I will help you."

When they hear this, and perhaps when you hear this, a typical
reaction might be, "What a jerk! Thanks a lot."

How much more impact could we have if we give ourselves
some space and time before launching into something new? I'm not
suggesting that everything needs to be forced into a waiting room
for six months, but I am suggesting that we seek to be countercultural when it comes to the inclination to start things as soon as
possible.

I don't want to be perceived as a guru on a mountaintop.
However, I want people to take the time needed to discern God's
direction. I want to see if the fire is still there and burning in a
month. In three months. In six months. I want to see if that passion
will stay lit over time.

I want to know if it's a calling and deep conviction rather than an emotional idea that will eventually go away. Why is this so important? Because I guarantee you will have setbacks, obstacles, barriers, opposition, criticism, complications, and disappointments. These problems are inevitable, but if we're fueled by a calling and conviction that this passion is what God desires of us, we will handle the storms that come our way.

God works in mysterious ways, but sometimes that waiting room is important. Nehemiah was eager and zealous, and wanted to move, but he actively practiced waiting.

My wish is that Christians, the church, and all those who are reading this book would take more time to listen, pray, and allow the injustices of the world to break us in lasting ways, as opposed to wanting to immediately make an impact. We should be about the marathon, not about the transactional sprint for instant justice gratification.

There was something spiritual, something mystical that took place in Nehemiah's life. God was using that time to mold him and prepare him for what was to come. This truly is countercultural.

In our world today we're often tempted to act quickly with our words and actions. Quick reaction, excitement, and initial passion may get attention out of the gate, but the work of discipleship is long and hard.

God Uses the Listeners

Life and discipleship is a marathon; it's not a sprint. We must take the long view of the work that God is doing. It requires time and commitment to be steadfast for the rest of our lives.

Shut up. Listen. Pray. That process will bless both you and whomever you are trying help. It opens up the possibility that God wants to teach you or change you.

In our culture today, listening has become a lost discipline, a discipline that needs to be recaptured. God does not always speak in the thunder and lightning. God often speaks in stillness and silence, on the wind.

Rather than speaking through blaring trumpets or powerful figures, God often chooses the foolish and weak to bring clarity to the wise, wealthy, and powerful. God chose to speak through a young, poor girl named Mary, who had great faith. God chose to speak to Elijah in the silence. We need to be encouraged to listen as Mary and Elijah did. We need to be still. As it requires courage to speak up, it also requires courage to shut up and listen. We need to learn to do both.

Allow the time, as Nehemiah did, for God to guide you into a season where He breaks you and remolds you. God cares about the work to which He calls us—and it's worth waiting to hear His voice before we begin. If we continue to listen to God, we may be sustained for the marathon of discipleship and doing the work of justice.

My year working as a janitor at Barnes and Noble was difficult, especially the time cleaning the ladies' room. But in that space, I learned again how to have a conversation with God. In that time, I found space for discernment. In that humbling and unexpected season, I had hours to think, discern, pray, and listen for our next steps in launching Quest.

Once the time finally came for us to hold our first informational gathering in our home, we wrote a summary of our vision and heart, and emailed it to a group of people. And we waited. We waited for God to show up in our apartment gathering. Thousands didn't come. Nor did hundreds. Seven people showed up.

But most important, God was present.

Chapter 5

BE TENACIOUS!

I was six years old, dressed in polyester, excited, anxious, and about to take my first trip on an airplane. The year was 1977. My two older brothers, Philip and Michael, were beside me as we followed my parents into the Seoul airport terminal, walking toward a jet bound for the United States.

As I walked down the Jetway, I didn't understand why people around me in the terminal were crying. What was wrong?

My parents—in their wisdom—thought it would be best not to tell me that we were moving. My brothers knew, but I had no clue. I was simply told that we were going on a trip. As a young boy, I was thrilled with the idea of getting on an airplane for the very first time. But when we got to the airport and I saw the waves of relatives there to see us off, all in tears, I understood—this was no vacation. And these relatives were saying good-bye. For good. We were moving to a very distant place called America.

Our family was poor—my parents had been poor their entire lives. They experienced years of life without having enough to eat, without a clear path to escape to something better.

Even though they did not know quite what to expect, my parents gambled on a move to the United States. They hoped that it might, at the least, offer their children an avenue to a better life. It probably took them months, maybe even years, to save the money to pay for our airplane tickets. I'm sure they called my mother's relatives in the United States as they were preparing to leave, asking, "Would you help us find an apartment?" "Could we work at your grocery store?"

My parents left behind everything they knew in Korea—their home, their community, their family—for the sake of their three boys. They imagined us going to school and growing up to become doctors and engineers.

Expectations were high that we would make something out of our lives.

When we landed at the airport in San Francisco, a new life awaited us, but I had no idea what that would be like. Because I was so young, there's not much I remember, but I do vividly remember clinging to my father's leg. The initial experience was frightening and surreal. To be honest, it was the very first time I'd ever seen white folks in real life. I couldn't stop staring at every single person that I saw. It was then I realized everything was going to be different.

Surprise!

My Family's Immigrant Story

People tell me that I work hard. They call me tenacious. I like the sound of "Tenacious E," but I haven't been able to get the nickname to stick … *not yet.*

If I have a tenacious bone in my body, I acquired it by watching my parents live steadfastly every day. Sung Wha, my mom, and Tok, my dad, embody commitment, perseverance, and tenacity.

They immigrated to this country knowing very little English, besides their broken English attempts at "Yes," "No," and "Tsank you." (They simply couldn't pronounce the "Th.") They had never been to the United States. They did not know the culture. But they knew that their boys needed the opportunities at a life that was not afforded to them. My parents learned numbers working the cash register at the family grocery store, the Royal Pine Market in San Francisco's Nob Hill neighborhood, and through hard work managed to purchase the same store years later.

At the age of six, I worked there too. So did my brothers—who were aged nine and twelve when we moved here. The American dream is possible, but as with anything important, it comes at a cost.

A week after arriving in the United States, I took the public bus alone as a first-grade student at Sherman Elementary School. My parents both needed to work, so they couldn't take me. At night, after being immersed in a new school, language, and culture, and after being called the occasional derogatory name, I stepped off the bus near the Royal Pine Market and began my job. No pay, of course. Working at the grocery store was just part of being a member of my immigrant family. I did a bit of everything, including stocking, cleaning, working the cash register, and delivering groceries to customers. Mind you, I was six.

I learned math quickly because I had to use the cash register. My parents never took a day off, with the exception of Sundays, and were always frugal … except when it came to our education. It was the primary thing in which they invested.

I don't know how they pulled it off, but a few months into their new life in the United States, they had saved up enough to buy a used piano. The Cho boys were going to learn how to play! My father recounted stories of his youth when he had to break into a church because he so desperately wanted to learn how to play piano—and he managed to teach himself. He didn't want his sons to break into anywhere to have a chance to enjoy music.

We started to save. We definitely had not yet arrived, but we were making progress.

About six months after we immigrated to the United States, a fire ripped through our apartment complex. I don't think that anybody died in the fire, but it was a traumatic experience and a major setback for our family. We escaped safely but lost nearly everything we owned, including the piano. We didn't know there was such a thing as renters insurance, so it was all just gone.

We were forced to start over, and for a season of our lives, it meant that our new home was the grocery store. We had a decrepit loft in the Royal Pine Market, which was not a pleasant place to live or sleep. It was dirty and cramped. I remember there was one nasty bed that we took turns sleeping on. Home was that bed and the floor of the loft, in the grocery store.

In one way you could say living at the store was more convenient for my parents because my mom opened the store at 7:00 a.m. and ended the day at 11:00 p.m. My father woke at five in the morning to head off to his job at a communications company and then worked at the store in the evening after his day job.

There were occasions during that difficult time when I heard my parents crying. They didn't want to scare us, but I quickly learned that my parents were human too. A couple of months after the fire, they had saved up enough, with some additional help from the extended family, to rent another apartment and start life over.

Again.

Shaped by Their Tenacity

We are, in many ways, products of our environments. I believe the tenacity of my parents shaped who I am and how I seek to live my life. I have learned this through my parents pushing forward, regardless of the obstacles ahead. I want to pass these lessons along to my kids, because I look at my kids and I see glimpses of what I am calling all of us to examine.

Please hear me out. I'm not trying to be that parent who bashes his own children in public. Nor am I trying to play into the stereotypes of Asian parents—the tiger moms and dads—made famous by Amy Chua, professor of law at Yale Law School and author of *Battle Hymn of the Tiger Mother*. Seriously, our kids are gracious, obedient, loving, and kindhearted—about 93 percent of the time. They thrive in school and have received their share of accolades. Okay, enough passive-aggressive boasting from me.

It's just that they reflect similar tendencies of so many in our culture today. In short, I question the fortitude and tenacity of our three children. As the pastor of an urban church in Seattle, where about 70 percent of our congregants are in their twenties and thirties, I wonder about the congregants' inner fortitude, perseverance, and tenacity. We live in a culture where it has become easy and tempting to simply quit. It is easier for us to move on to the next thing, the next relationship, the next profession, the next calling, the next church, or the next conviction.

Why? Simply because we can.

We live in a culture of opportunity in which we're encouraged to try new things, which is good, but I worry about that leading to a sense of entitlement. As a result, we think we deserve everything. We think others owe us. We think our parents owe us. We think our churches owe us. We think that our governments owe us. We think *God* Himself owes us.

If we're not careful, we won't grow in our personal or leadership development. Our maturity will be stunted, and we'll shrug off the responsibility of owning our decisions and pursuing our convictions. When we live with privilege and entitlement and a lack of perseverance and tenacity, it's tempting to simply move on to the next new thing.

As I consider my kids—in their present and future—these questions often come to mind: What are their oppositions? What will test them? What will provoke their sense of perseverance and build character? What will challenge their sense of entitlement and privilege?

For my parents, extreme poverty and war served those roles. They couldn't avoid it. Korea was torn apart by war, and even in the late seventies, Korea was still in the process of rebuilding. Every city of any size had been destroyed or heavily damaged in the war. The economy hobbled along. So many people barely survived, even fifteen years after the war ended. My folks struggled through it and found a path out of it. It was clearly not an easy road.

My father was only six when he and his family fled from what is now called North Korea. They fled in the middle of the night because of the persecution they faced for being some of the first followers of Jesus in their small village. Little did they know that a war called the Korean War (which has technically never ended) would begin and ravage their people, divide them into two countries, and separate many families.

I vividly remember my father telling me that his job as a young boy was to scour through the garbage from restaurants and collect eggshells.

Eggshells? I know.

I was puzzled myself when he first shared this story with me.

He gathered dozens of eggshells and then took them to my grandmother, who helped him grind them into fine powder. She put the powder into boiling water and created a soup base or something equivalent to Korean milk—a source of calcium for the family.

For me, the reality that helped shape my character more than anything else was being an immigrant in America. It was hard being ridiculed, laughed at, and mocked. I was often bullied and got into many fights. I may or may not have lost many of those fights. The experiences forced me to push beyond obstacles, tested my perseverance, and built my tenacity.

In the sixth grade I was voted the shiest student in my school. For numerous years I struggled through self-esteem issues and a lack of confidence, primarily because of my inability to speak English and also for the simple but profound reason that I was seen as an "other."

During high school I decided that I would conquer my fears and considered what would be the most challenging thing I could do. The answer was theater. I don't know if you've ever seen or read William Shakespeare's *A Midsummer Night's Dream.* Not to brag, but after auditioning, I was awarded the very prestigious role of Wall. (Okay, it wasn't very prestigious, but it was a role nevertheless.) As Wall, I was used as a literal barrier for the lovers, Pyramus and Thisbe. They would talk and kiss through my fingers. I had a couple of lines, including:

> In this same interlude it doth befall
> That I, one Snout by name, present a wall. (5.1)

Impressive, right? I crushed it. #BestWallEver

Even in my tiny role as Wall, I started to outgrow my shyness and overcome my fear of speaking. I was pushing myself to learn the language, learn the culture.

If it's not poverty or immigration, what will be the opposition my children face? It's not that I intentionally want them to suffer or face opposition, but I worry when many of their problems are first-world problems.

Why can't we have a new video-game console?

Why can't we have cable TV?

Why can't we have a bigger house?

Why can't we _____?

Not to say that we don't shower them with gifts when we can, but it is a concern we should all have. We live in a culture of abundance and entitlement. It is really easy for us to shift. It's easy for us to make decisions, and it is easy for us to quit. If we go through this cycle of always quitting or moving on to the next shiny thing, and fail to endure, we will never experience the joy of hard times. We will never enjoy the fruit of learning, pushing, preserving, and being tenacious through the journey of our callings and convictions.

There's wisdom from these words from the apostle Paul: "Not only so, but we also glory in our sufferings, because we know that suffering produces perseverance; perseverance, character; and character, hope" (Rom. 5:3–4).

After my parents immigrated to the States, their work schedules were unbelievable. My father *left* the home at five in the morning to head off to work. My mother woke at six to get the grocery store open by seven. They would stay at the grocery store until eleven o'clock at night. That meant getting home around midnight. Most nights, they might have slept five hours. Oh, and did I mention the Royal Pine Market was open on Saturdays too?

These are about one-hundred-hour weeks. Who does that?

As a teenager, I continued to work at the grocery store. I was bitter, upset. I compared my life to my friends who were out playing and having fun. I wasn't always happy about this comparison.

I thank God that we don't have to endure this today, but the older I get, I look back with appreciation at the tenacity and sacrifice of my parents. They essentially gave their lives for the future of their children.

You don't learn these kinds of lessons on the Internet.

Be About the Marathon

When I think back on anything important that I have pursued in my life, it has been difficult. Nothing has come easy. Everything has taken longer to come together than I expected. Often the delay between dreaming my dreams and having them realized can be measured in years.

I think back on the commitments that I've made, the passions I've chased, and I consider the many times during those pursuits when I have actively and honestly considered quitting. I have wanted to throw in the towel. Cash in my chips. Give up.

I say that as an admission. I am human. But I have come to a realization after seeing some of my dreams finally come together.

This is what I know:

I believe we should be about the marathon and not about instant gratification. We don't need one-hit wonders; we need steady and faithful engagement. We need people who are faithful. People who are tenacious. People who don't give up. These people are few and far between. But they can truly change the world.

This critique is not something that is exclusive to any generation. This is for those people who are breathing and alive right now. I see this as a cultural problem that is larger than any generation. Today, it's just so easy.

Easy to change.

Easy to quit.

Easy to abandon ship.

Easy to file for a divorce online.

So easy to do whatever.

We can explain away everything with our rationalizing, theologizing, Bible interpreting, and emotional justifying.

I'm not trying to say that emotions aren't important, but emotion shouldn't be our sole and exclusive guide in all situations. Emotions can guide us, and they can also lead us astray. They can contradict my convictions.

Have you ever heard this kind of promise: "Three easy steps to achieving all your dreams!"?

Anyone who suggests such ludicrous fallacies is simply lying to you. There's a cost to pursuing your dreams, visions, and convictions. And there's a cost to following Jesus.

This is discipleship.

Hang in There, Friends

Over and over in Scripture, we read that if we trust God—if we really, really believe—we will get rich and have an easy life. Oh, hang on, I was just reading one of those prosperity theology, name-it-and-claim-it books and got distracted.

No, in fact we see that—*if anything*—life often becomes more challenging when we choose to follow Christ. Bluntly, following Jesus will probably mess you up. How? Following Jesus brings a dramatic change to our lives, plans, ambitions, hopes, and plans for world domination. While following Jesus does bring blessing, including the blessing of being in relationship with our Creator, we learn quickly that the kingdom of God beats to a different rhythm from the kingdom of this world. And if you're not convinced of this, just read Jesus's Sermon on the Mount.

One of my favorite passages in the Bible is in Acts 2, particularly verses 42 through 47, which talk about how the early church endured and grew. Here's an excerpt:

> They devoted themselves to the apostles' teaching
> and to fellowship, to the breaking of bread and
> to prayer.... And the Lord added to their number
> daily those who were being saved.

There are a lot of books out there about self-help, self-growth, self-whatever. Here we see there was no secret recipe, no shortcut, just evidence of long-term commitment. They devoted themselves to study, fellowship, breaking bread, and prayer. Do you know what I think the most important element was? I think the most important element was not *what* they did, but rather the devotion itself.

Read verse 42 again.

They *devoted* themselves.

A lot of people ask how they should change their church to make it grow. They ask, "What new strategies should we employ?"

Pretty simple, actually.

They were steadfast. They cared. They devoted themselves to one another, to Christ, and to the building of God's kingdom.

Are we devoted?

Through the Storm

Do you remember the gripping story from Mark 4:35–41 when Jesus told His disciples, "Let us go over to the other side [of the lake]"?

This is a mind-bending story.

The disciples, some of them professional fishermen, evaluated the conditions and decided it was safe to go across the lake. Once they were on the water, Jesus went below deck and took a nap. We know where the story went from there. While Jesus slept, an epic storm nearly capsized the boat. There are a lot of fascinating elements of this story.

For one, Jesus initiated this life-threatening journey. No one spotted the danger, and Jesus didn't point it out in advance. The fishing experts among them, Peter in particular, said it was safe to sail. You can't predict all the storms that will come in to your life, no matter how much of an expert you are. When it's all said and done, you do not have full control of your life. Had I known that our two and a half years of simplifying our lives, saving, and selling would have produced some of the most difficult times of our life, I may not have started One Day's Wages. Looking back on the pain we endured to plant a church, I don't know that I would've started Quest.

Jesus allows challenges to present themselves in our lives. But the story doesn't stop there: During this epic storm, Jesus was asleep. But there was also something very important going on. It's the reality that Jesus was present with them during the storm. And He is with us. We may not like the posture that Jesus takes, but it doesn't take away from the truth that Jesus is present.

And this is the gospel: The good news is not merely that Jesus saves but that Jesus is with us. The promise of the gospel isn't the health and wealth we often hear through erroneous prosperity theology, but that in all situations, God is with us.

He does not leave us.

The story continues. Jesus woke up and taught a lesson, but the storm didn't necessarily end at that moment. It actually continued. Jesus allowed this faith-stretching danger because He wanted His disciples to grow. He wants to build our trust, which will happen only if we weather the storms. We have to endure.

Let's not be so quick to curse the storms and abandon our ships. Let's not be so quick to change course when we encounter difficulties and setbacks. Sometimes we can learn our best lessons when we endure storms.

> *Smooth seas do not make skillful sailors.*
> —African proverb

Some Faithful Guys Teach Us a Lesson

In Luke 5 we read about what most scholars speculate to be four friends who encounter a man who was paralyzed. They felt compassion for the man and wanted to bring him to Jesus for healing.

Let's be real here—it probably wasn't an easy task. We don't know how long or how far they carried this person. We don't know the conditions of the road or path. We have no idea how heavy this man was, but to carry a grown man who could not help himself move was, and is, no easy task. In short, it was a commitment.

So these guys carried this man to the home where Jesus was speaking, believing that Jesus could do something to help. When they arrived, they saw that the home was packed. There was a huge crowd. Standing room only. There was absolutely no way in. Story over. They had every reason to give up.

Put yourself in this situation. Imagine if it were you. You see the huge crowd. You're tired. You've just carried a grown dude for some fair distance. You probably say, "Sorry, dude," and give up. Fair enough. So you hold up your phone, snap a selfie of yourself frowning, with the invalid and the crowd in the background of the picture, then cross-post it to Facebook and Twitter with this comment:

> Way too crowded. Maybe next time. #TryingToHelp
> #Invalid #Jesus #YOLO

You'd get lots of likes, several affirming comments to your post, and seven retweets. The story could've ended there. We would all applaud with a polite golf clap. We would say, "I don't blame you. You did what you could." Isn't that such a common saying nowadays? *You did what you could.*

Sometimes we underestimate not just what we can do in our lives but what God can do in our lives. These guys did not give up. They had faith that God could act, that He could heal. They were compelled by their compassion for this man who understood the pain of being marginalized, ostracized, and ignored. They considered their options and came up with a solution they probably thought was a bit crazy at first. If they couldn't bring this paralyzed man through the door, they'd lower him down into the home *through the roof.*

Once they decided that lowering a man in from the ceiling would be a good idea, they needed to figure out how to do it. While I'm no expert on house structures of the first century in Israel, they likely had to walk up some steep, narrow stairs on the side of the home and then hoist him up onto the roof. Together they lifted 150 to 200 pounds of unwieldy weight. Once they figured that out and did it, they then had to dismantle the roof itself. I hope the homeowner had insurance. Once the roof had a sizable hole in it, the man had to be lowered into the room. Imagine the yelling and commotion from within the crowded home. Everyone in the room looked up at the roof.

And then, of course, Jesus healed their friend and commended their faith.

What a moment.

This story inspires me for several reasons.

These men had compassion. They cared. They saw the invalid as someone worthy of attention.

They had faith in Jesus. This was fairly early in Jesus's ministry, and I'm certain that these men still had many questions about Jesus, but what they knew, heard, felt, and experienced was enough for them to have faith in Him.

They worked together to make this happen. When I say we've got to be tenacious, I'm not suggesting that we have to be tenacious by ourselves. Sometimes we've got to look for like-minded, like-hearted, and similarly tenacious people, and either join them or recruit them to our cause.

Their creativity inspires me. They probably had to convince people that though it seemed crazy, they could do it. They didn't quit. They had a goal in mind. It may not have been pretty. They might've said a few choice words along the way. They certainly messed up a roof. Maybe they dropped the man at one point. I'm sure they were sweaty, but they believed that his life mattered.

Maybe it seems kind of self-centered, but when Jesus looked up and saw them opening up the roof, the Bible says that He saw their faith. The faith of the men helping. Then Jesus told the disabled man, "Your sins are forgiven" (v. 20).

Now that's a better ending to the story. And imagine this tweet instead:

> We did it! Jesus saw the man, healed him, forgave him! #Thankful #PraiseJesus #RaiseTheRoof

It's the Coffee, Stupid

When I consider perseverance in my own life, I think of the Q Café, which is an example of reinvention over time and not giving up on a dream. I know this café may not last forever, but since our church built this café in 2002 (when Quest was less than one year old), I marvel at how much it has blessed our community.

I don't know if you know this, but there are a few other coffee shops in Seattle other than the Q Café. Most notably, there is this dinky coffee-shop chain called Starbucks headquartered in our city. Too early to tell at this writing, but it might really take off. You may want to buy some of its stock. Just remember, you heard it from me first.

When I became a pastor, I wanted to do something more than just open a traditional church. It made sense to start a coffee shop, because we are living in a post-Christian world, where people aren't just going to come to a Sunday service.

We wanted to be a presence in our neighborhood. Somehow we wanted to become a living room, a third space, a public meeting place. We wanted to become a good neighbor. So, we asked ourselves a couple of simple questions: How can we bless our neighbors? How can we bless our city?

This gave birth to the Q Café—a neighborhood nonprofit café featuring espresso and tea, art, live music, and community events. At the beginning of its existence, the café was also our church building on Sundays. With only 4,500 square feet that comprised our café, offices, and classrooms, we used every single square foot. Every single one, every single day.

So, let me back up for a moment here … because the idea for the Q Café goes back a long way. After my parents sold their grocery-store business, it wasn't that long before my mother opened up another small business. This time, it was a coffee shop. She named it Jane's Café because her English name is Jane. I had suggested she call it Eugene's Café or I Love My Sons Café, but she named it after herself. I know. Selfish.

I helped at the coffee shop when I was on breaks during college. Having observed her from afar, I thought I had a good grasp on running a coffee shop. The reality was I had merely a romanticized view of the coffee shop and never grasped how difficult it was to sustain a small business until Q Café.

When we launched Q Café, we didn't have a real strategic plan but more of a romanticized vision. It was painful. I had a good idea, and a church that was willing to go along with me, but it wasn't good enough. We didn't take the time to pray, discern, listen, and wait; instead we rushed into this endeavor.

I learned the hard way that when it's all said and done, everyone is still a consumer with a consumer mentality. Nonprofit or not, if your product sucks, nobody is going to come back. We thought that if we skimped and cut corners to save valuable financial resources, it would still work out because we were a nonprofit café, art gallery, rental space, and music venue, and pouring 10 percent of our sales back into other nonprofits in the Seattle area. But it didn't work.

Part of our problem was that we used Folgers instant coffee. Not really, but we initially opted for cheaper espresso beans because, well, they were cheaper. We looked for suppliers and roasters who would give us the best deal, not the best quality. We also didn't come alongside our staff with proper training from our roasters, and that made a difference in the quality of the drinks that our customers received.

Might I add that the Q Café was never about coffee (talk about dreaming big). When it opened, we had a children's program nearly every week; a computer lab for senior citizens in the neighborhood; live music; monthly art gallery exhibits featuring local artists; event bookings; homeless engagement, including connecting people with basic case management and clothes distribution.

What did this all look like?

Here's how it worked: The baristas would make a drink, then run to the back of the room and find a pair of jeans for a homeless client. They would literally run across the café, find 34-waist pants and two pairs of socks, and run back across the room to pull shots for a double caramel macchiato.

We had a big dream, and it was a good dream.

But it was also a nonrealistic dream. I learned the painful way that the reality is you can't do everything. We can be informed and educated about many things, but we can only go deep in a few things.

The person who tries to do everything will do nothing well, and this was certainly the case with Q Café. Rather, it's best to do a few things and to do them well with kindness and love.

In my attempts to do everything, we sort of messed up on the most essential aspect of Q Café. Coffee? Oh yeah. That.

Sort of important for a coffee shop. Just saying.

I still remember the hurt and embarrassment of getting feedback on a couple of occasions to the effect of: "Your coffee sucks." It was painful when it came from folks in my own church, and especially painful when it came from my wife!

We didn't want to mess this up. The Q Café was the realization of what I felt God was calling our church to do in the community. So with blessings from our leadership, I took the unprecedented step as the chief barista (yes, a title I gave myself) to shut down the café for two months to revamp, reorganize, and reboot.

We decided that we needed to recommit ourselves to the art of coffee. The art of espresso.

Yes, there were a lot of things we wanted to do as a coffee shop. We wanted to be a great rental space, a good community space, a good music venue, a good art gallery, and a place for people to have a safe encounter with a church. But for a coffee shop not to excel in coffee would be an oxymoron.

We made numerous changes. We changed roasters. We decided to make sure every barista went through proper training: No one could touch the machine unless he or she had been trained. We made sure the baristas understood that coffee was an art, a craft, and a skill. We decided that if there's one thing we should do well as a coffee shop—and this may blow your mind—we had to do coffee really well. Without that, we had no credibility to do anything else. We also rethought everything else about the café.

If I could do it all over again, I would focus on the essentials and grow from there. When I tell people that they can't do everything, it's not because I'm trying to sound like a pessimist, but rather I'm simply trying to be honest with my scars. I have lived and walked that road of trying to do too much, or everything, and as a result, I burned many people out.

We refined our strategy, developed a long-term vision, and positioned ourselves to be a light to the neighborhood. We just needed to listen, pray, and discern.

Thank God we did.

Since we paused and reopened in 2008, I have never heard people say that our coffee is horrible. I've not heard anybody say that in the past few years. Even my wife loves the coffee now. She usually orders the extra-hot caramel latte with soy milk, ristretto shots with golden crema, and extra smooth foam. Yes, we're all coffee snobs in Seattle. Today the Q Café is one of the highest-ranked coffee shops in the city. We don't get the traffic of Starbucks, and the reality is that we still have to be creative to pay all our bills, but I know that we're fulfilling our vision of being a good neighbor.

We've hosted hundreds and hundreds of live music shows, including up-and-coming local and national artists. We have rotating art gallery showings, weekly open mike, and we've hosted rentals, benefit shows, weddings, parties, and film screenings. We've also hosted both Democratic and Republican Party caucuses, city council meetings, and served as a meeting location for Gamblers Anonymous and Alcoholics Anonymous. Professors from local universities and colleges bring their classes here for occasional field trips.

We had a vision. We were tested. We had the courage to be tenacious and press on. It warms my heart, because even though we're not blowing up the bottom line, we are fully living our vision of who we want to be. I am so glad we didn't give up.

Now, I'm gonna go and enjoy my Americano.

Let's Go Together

There's a moment from a few years ago that will stick with me until the day I die. It's regarding Sung Wha, my mother.

Minhee and I were at a point of transition, between working at an ethnic Korean church in the northern suburbs of Seattle called Lynnwood and launching Quest in urban Seattle. As I shared earlier, I was in desperate need of a job. I had a mortgage to pay. A pregnant wife. A kid at home.

Then, praise God, after months without work, I finally landed a job.

My mom was in between jobs at this point in her life. She was in her late fifties, but she had such bad knees and degenerative hips that it was, and is, difficult for her to walk. My mom is like a human barometer—when a storm is coming and when it rains, her hips throb. Although my parents lived in San Francisco, she was visiting us in Seattle to encourage us in this difficult season.

As I prepared to go to work one early morning, I walked downstairs to put on my jacket and shoes, and forgot that my mother woke up early every morning to pray. In fact, she had been praying for months that I would find the right job.

"Eugene, where are you going?" she said when she saw me.

I hadn't told my mother the news that I had just recently been hired for the janitorial gig at Barnes and Noble. I chose not to because I thought she and my father would be devastated. I didn't want them to think that after laboring, sacrificing, and doing so much for us over all those years that their son had failed them.

But I couldn't lie to her, so eventually I told my mom that I got a job and was going to work.

"Great! What job? What are you doing?"

I hesitated.

"Um, I'm working at Barnes and Noble as their custodian," I said finally.

Without asking another question, my mother got up from the dining table where she had been reading her Bible and praying. She walked slowly toward me.

To be honest, I was a little scared from my memories as a teen-ager of her being a disciplinarian. She approached me, then walked past me without saying a word, and I realized she was headed toward the closet. She opened the closet door, put on her jacket, turned around and said to me (in Korean), "Eugene, let's go together. I will help you."

This moment perfectly captures her heart. The heart of my parents: Loving. Willing to help. Willing to walk with me. Tenacious and devoted to the end.

Chapter 6

ASKING THE HARD QUESTIONS: SELF-EXAMINATION

Let's be honest here: We are into ourselves. We might not want to admit it, but if we started a fan page for ourselves, we'd click "like." In fact, I think I did exactly that when I started my Facebook page.

We love holding up our smartphones and snapping selfies. We love telling people where we're at, what we're doing, and what we're feeling.

> Look at me! Look at this food that I'm about to devour! Look at my clothes! Look at my hot wife! Look at my stud muffin of a husband! Look at my [fill in the blank]!

You do it. She does it. He does it. I do it. We all do it.

We care about how we look. We care about our image and thus the projection of our image online. We care about what others think of us. But when does self-promotion become harmful—not just to ourselves but to others?

Today, justice and the idea of justice have become trendy, like joining a band in the eighties. I don't even know how to play an instrument, and I was in a band back then. Now, I'm not saying that I'd rather *injustice* be trendy, but our culture of narcissism begs an important question: Why are we doing what we're doing?

If you want to change the world, then why, exactly, do you want to do that?

It's a question I encourage you to ask yourself—not just once but as an ongoing self-examination. I've had to ask myself that question, and the answer is often troubling.

Is this for my own selfishness?

Is this for my own greed? For my own happiness?

Why do I want to be involved in the work of justice?

Why do I feel called to do this work?

There is good reason to ask these questions. *Self-reflection matters.*

When all is said and done, after we've respectively launched our new project, vision, or idea, our new idea won't be new anymore. The shine will wear off. The glamour will fade away. The trend will not be as trendy.

We do what we do because we love God and we love the people whom God loves. We love the things that God loves and what reflects the character of God. We do justice not because it is sexy, glamorous, or trendy, but because God loves justice. Justice isn't a clothing accessory we wear when it becomes fashionable, but rather it is something we live into because it reflects the character of God.

Examine your heart.

Getting Real in Nebraska

My family and I go to Nebraska for two weeks every summer. Some people think we're crazy.

"*Nebraska?* What's in Nebraska? Do you know anyone in Nebraska? And you are driving there from Seattle?"

Yes, it's a long journey.

Yes, we take our three kids with us in a van.

Yes, it's more than three thousand miles round-trip.

Yes, I do allow bathroom breaks for the kids.

And yes, corn tastes better in Nebraska.

For the Cho family, our annual pilgrimage to a small town in Nebraska has been one of the richest experiences we've enjoyed together. It's a time to simply be a family. We're outside of good cell-phone reception range, in a quiet place where we can disconnect, be together, and listen to God. In this small town, we stay in a place with no television, no cable, no Internet, no smartphones, and no Korean dramas on Netflix.

It doesn't hurt that a fishing rod, several lakes, and many beautiful eight-pound bass are involved as well (catch and release, of course).

You might think I'm crazy, but one of my favorite parts of our family pilgrimage is the hours spent on the road. As the saying goes, it's not always about the destination; it's about the journey.

Hours blur together as we cruise down the highway. We stare at the horizon as farm fields race past.

And as we drive, Minhee and I talk quietly.

It's not unusual for the two of us to talk for hours, with the kids zonked out in the back of the van. They've already played the license-plate game. Traffic is light and at times nonexistent along the long, straight roads of Wyoming. So it's just us, the road ahead, and the twilight sky.

At times like these we have our best conversations.

I remember a few years ago when we were still thinking through the launch of One Day's Wages. In prayer, we came up with the idea, feeling convicted and inspired by God to act on our compassion and advocacy for the poor. We spent hours and days in the car on our road trips, talking about this vision.

My wife knows me better than anyone else. She knows my gifts and strengths, and also all my weaknesses. She knows my imperfections, my brokenness, and my depravity. The reality of who I am has been fully exposed to her, and vice versa. There is something provocative and unnerving when my wife looks over at me intently, as only a wife and trained therapist can, and challenges me.

It was the summer of 2009, and we thought about and prayed about our plans to launch our nonprofit. Although we had received praise and encouragement for our plans to start One Day's Wages, we had also received our share of criticism and skepticism, especially at the beginning. And some of the criticism was convicting.

One question we frequently heard, which was entirely fair, asked why we felt as if we needed to start something new, rather than just donating to an existing organization.

So when my wife dug into these issues, it was incredibly sensitive, perhaps even painful, but definitely valuable. On that road trip, and on several occasions as we came closer to launching ODW, she asked me questions I wrestled with, such as, "Are you sure this is not all about you? Are we sure that this is not all about us?"

Without being willing to explore our motives, to be deeply introspective, to give permission to trusted friends to ask the hard questions, how can we possibly act with honesty and integrity? How can we know that our care, generosity, advocacy, and pursuit of justice are not just a show?

Consider the wisdom in these words from Tim Keller: "Doing justice, then, requires constant sustained reflection and circumspection. If you are a Christian, and you refrain from committing adultery or using profanity or missing church, but you don't do the hard work of thinking through how to do justice in every area of life—you are failing to live justly and righteously."[1]

It is out of love that we challenge our brothers and sisters, husbands and wives, sons and daughters, and colaborers to live in the way of Christ. If we are not in relationship with others seeking God, how can we possibly ask such questions?

We will only accept a dialogue about such things if we have decided that asking the hard questions is important. Without asking difficult questions, without exploring the ramifications of our actions, we can hurt ourselves, hurt others, and do a disservice to the ministry or work we want to share with the world.

When emotion is fleeting, when convictions wane, we need to know that we have asked ourselves the hard questions.

My Confession

As I have said, much of this book is a confession, especially this chapter. I have embarked on many initiatives and have wrestled with the "why" every time. Why did I feel the need to plant a church, to start the café and music venue, start a humanitarian organization, or write this book?

These convictions came through research, prayer, and a growing sense that these projects were going to be hard. I felt drawn and compelled to such endeavors. I felt peace and conviction, and I felt that God's call was to surrender and obey.

The inspirations I had to start a church, open a coffee shop, and launch a humanitarian organization are not unique inclinations. They have been done before. What was unique is that I discerned that God had called me to contribute in these specific areas.

I'm sure most folks who question these initiatives ask with good intentions. While everyone should check their motivations and vision, I am thankful for the folks who went before us who chose to move forward in conviction and calling—even when asked those very same questions.

So ask the hard questions. Be wise and discerning. And may we all have the courage to respond faithfully, prayerfully, and courageously to these convictions when they are questioned.

When I think about courage, I often ponder the life and leadership of Martin Luther King Jr. On my desk is a quote that I read often. It's a reminder that while injustice, hatred, and evil exist in the world, good exists alongside them:

> When evil men plot, good men must plan. When
> evil men burn and bomb, good men must build and
> bind. When evil men shout ugly words of hatred,
> good men must commit themselves to the glories
> of love. Where evil men would seek to perpetuate
> an unjust status quo, good men must seek to bring
> into being a real order of justice.[2]

Indeed, we need good women and men who commit to the glories of love, to the work of the kingdom.

The Reward for Self-Examination

So what is in it for people who take the time to consider their motives? What do they get out of this process of self-examination?

For one thing, it means they will have a better chance of making their intentions amount to something. Taking time to reflect and examine motives helps us ensure that the work is not all about us, but about something of deeper significance.

Allowing space to pray, reflect, and ask the hard questions will help us to be more faithful. It helps us to form a deeper foundation for the work itself. It helps us to do our work in a more honest, dignified, and God-honoring way.

I love the instructions the apostle Paul gave the church in Philippi:

> Finally, brothers and sisters, whatever is true,
> whatever is noble, whatever is right, whatever is

pure, whatever is lovely, whatever is admirable—if
anything is excellent or praiseworthy—think about
such things. (Phil. 4:8)

I want to affirm and encourage people who want to do good
things. I also want to challenge them not to accept a plan that is
mediocre when it could be excellent. I want to better prepare them.
I want to set them up to have a major impact. I want to set them up
for faithful work.

If we are motivated and fueled by things that might not resonate
with God's kingdom, we can get burned out with the work and hurt
people. We'll end up doing much harm along the way.

In an age of excessive self-broadcasting, the discipline of self-
examination and introspection are the keys to wisdom and balance.

Does God want us to ask hard questions?

Of course! God wants everything in our lives, including the
examination of our motives, to give us something deeper. When we
offer Christ everything, He offers hope and a future that we could
not dream up or achieve on our own.

Something both frustrating and refreshing about Christ is the
way He asked questions of people rather than simply handing out
instructions. Jesus ushered in a new kind of faith—less about rules
and more about motive and heart.

Asking questions demands reflection. Asking questions just
might change our opinions. Asking questions helps bring depth into
who we are and the road ahead.

I love the relationship that developed between Jesus and Simon
Peter. In the gospel of Matthew, when Jesus asked His disciples who

people said He was, they offered various responses. "Some say John the Baptist; others say Elijah; and still others ... one of the prophets" (Matt. 16:14). Then Jesus narrowed the question to Peter:

> "But what about you?" he asked. "Who do you say I am?"
>
> Simon Peter answered, "You are the Messiah, the Son of the living God."
>
> Jesus replied, "Blessed are you, Simon son of Jonah, for this was not revealed to you by flesh and blood, but by my Father in heaven. (vv. 15–17)

It's easy to answer a question posed generally but more difficult and convicting to answer a question when it is directed at us individually.

I also love the question Jesus poses in the gospel of John to a man who's been paralyzed and thus seen as "disabled" for thirty-eight years, collecting money at the edge of the pool at Bethesda.

Jesus asked him, "Do you want to get well?" (John 5:6).

At the outset of reading this story, I thought, *What a horrible question—how insensitive are You, Jesus? You're talking to a man who cannot walk and who's been disabled for thirty-eight years. Isn't it obvious what he wants? You're Jesus. Shouldn't You know what he needs?*

However, when you ponder the question and reflect on the context of this man's life, this is a very profound and appropriate question.

The man doesn't answer the question; he begins to make excuses about why he hasn't gotten better. He tells Jesus that other people always cut in line in front of him. Later in the passage, Jesus catches up with the man he has healed and instructs him to stop sinning. We can only imagine the details, but it's clear that Jesus knew the man's heart. The danger of making excuses is that eventually we start believing in them.

Do we want to get well?

Let me rephrase the question: Do *you* really want to get well?

Do you want to impact other people's lives? Do you want your life to be changed? Or do you just want to make a name for yourself? Is this about God's glory, or is it about self-promotion?

What is your conviction? Do you really want your dream to happen? That's the question I pose to many with whom I meet. If it is in the context of marriage counseling, I say, "Do *you* really want this marriage to work?" If the individual can't say yes to that, he or she won't make progress. We must ask those hard questions in our own lives to shape a path for actual change.

Do you really want to get well?

These questions matter because we'll soon learn—one way or another—that there's a cost to discipleship. There's a cost to following Jesus. There's a cost to living generously. There's a cost to seeking justice. There's a cost to living sacrificially. There's a cost to obedience.

So put aside those whimsical, flippant answers. Instead, ask yourself the hard questions. Engage in self-reflection. Invite those you trust to ask and engage in those questions and conversations too. This process helps you examine your sense of calling, trust, obedience, and reckless surrender to what God wants you to do.

Eugene the Dream Destroyer

If you don't know who you are, you risk burnout, shortcuts, and the possibility that your good intentions will harm others. I don't care how old you are, how young you are, or how long you've been doing the work, the risks are all the same.

When people come and speak to me about their dreams, I do want to encourage them. I don't want to be known as the destroyer of dreams, aka "Eugene the Dream Destroyer." I truly want to encourage and affirm but also sharpen and deepen people in their dreams and convictions. This is not a matter of doing justice, but *how* we do justice. In that spirit I also feel burdened to test their zeal. I feel that I need to push back and ask them some hard questions.

If you proclaim that you're going to change the world, I hope you've taken the time to pray, listen, wait, discern, engage in self-reflection, and create a good plan. You might disappoint your sponsors and donors if that hasn't happened. You might even hurt those you're trying to help.

I'd like to share a poignant story of a couple of friends who shared their "I want to change the world" journey with me. They gave me permission to share their story, in hopes that it might help others ask the hard questions.

After visiting a particular village in a country in Africa, they were sincerely moved and convicted by what they saw. They met with many of the villagers and the village leaders, and learned that education for the children of the village was difficult because of the lack of financial resources to purchase uniforms and basic school supplies. Knowing that education changes lives, these friends promised the villagers that they would go back to the United States, raise money and awareness, and finance the education of *all* the children of the *entire* village. Parents in the village rejoiced and subsequently shared the news with their children, who then also rejoiced. These two friends were applauded as heroes. There were many photos taken with smiling children during their brief two-week mission trip to this village.

Now, to clarify, there were approximately 150 children in the village. This was no small endeavor.

Gulp.

These well-intentioned friends started a nonprofit when they got back to their respective homes, with the goal of funding education for the children of an entire village—*all the way through high school.*

Double gulp.

They contacted their family, friends, and churches to mobilize support. They hosted a couple of fund-raisers and managed to raise several thousand dollars.

You can guess the end of the story.

They couldn't deliver their promise to the village, the families, or the children. In the end they only raised enough funds for *some* to go to school, resulting in families in this village fighting, arguing, and debating which kids of which families should first utilize the scholarship funds. It became contentious and caused great division and strife in the village.

They had no mechanism, no infrastructure, and no accountability.

Ultimately, these friends learned some major lessons, but in the process, they hurt and disappointed the very people they were trying to help.

Three (or 3,627) Cups of Tea

You may remember the story in Greg Mortenson and David Oliver Relin's bestselling book, *Three Cups of Tea*. It documents in vivid detail Mortenson's experience in the mountains of Pakistan, being rescued by villagers after an attempt to climb the world's second-tallest mountain, K2.

Inspired by the hospitality of the villagers and convicted by what he saw in their community, Mortenson, along with a Silicon Valley entrepreneur, founded a nonprofit called Central Asia Institute to build schools in Afghanistan and Pakistan.

The goal of the nonprofit was to promote peace in Taliban-inhabited communities through education and relationships.

The problem was that after the book became a huge bestseller, much of the story was proven to be false.

Several independent investigators, including bestselling author Jon Krakauer, uncovered major factual problems with the book.[3] In the book, Mortenson told in great detail how he had come to terms with death after being abducted by members of the Taliban. That story, the subsequent story of villagers taking him in after the climb, and many other details were fabricated, according to various investigations. There are also lawsuits pending about financial mismanagement of the charity he started.[4]

As a result, the coauthor of the book, David Relin, committed suicide. He found it impossible to find work after the scandal erupted, and he tragically ended his life by stepping in front of a freight train near his home in Oregon.[5]

Wow. The ramifications of staying true are huge. To others and yourself.

Today, we believe stories change the world. Yes, they do. But by emphasizing that so much, we place the art of storytelling on a pedestal. At times we may feel tempted to manipulate the story so that it becomes more attractive, or dare I say it, marketable.

Marketable for what?

Some try to manipulate a story to sell products, solicit more donations, build our platforms, or grow our tribe.

It's true that one can tell a story in a variety of ways. But for Mortenson to entirely fabricate a story that the Taliban had captured him is clearly an example of deceitfulness and manipulation. That's not a story open to interpretation or to the art of storytelling. To flat out make up stories to inspire people? That's called lying. That's attempting to tell a good story instead of the truth. Huge difference.

Consider the damage caused by this one story. Consider the damage to the lives of Relin and Mortenson, the damage to the charity Mortenson started, the damage to nonprofit credibility everywhere.

In the days after the scandal was uncovered, *New York Times* columnist Nicholas Kristof wrote:

> The furor over Greg's work breaks my heart. And the greatest loss will be felt not by those of us whose hero is discredited, nor even by Greg himself, but by countless children in Afghanistan who now won't get an education after all. But let's not forget that even if all the allegations turn out to be true, Greg has still built more schools and transformed more children's lives than you or I ever will.[6]

That may be true. But imagine what could have been done if they had lived out a good story and simply written the truth instead of making up a story.

Don't Just Tell a Good Story; Live a Better Story

We need to be teachable. We need to be humble. We need to start from a posture to learn from others. There's a reason why I started One Day's Wages later in my life. I'm not sure that I had the maturity when I was younger to pause, weigh, discern, and take my time. I was in such a rush to do things. In my younger years, I confess I was enamored of making a name for myself.

I was thirty-nine when I started ODW. Over the years I've had my share of successes and scars. But I want to be as teachable as possible and learn from what others are doing. I want to see where God is already working. I've come to learn—at times in painful ways—that long before I ever arrived on the scene, God's been at work.

Long before we started Quest, God was at work in Seattle. God was at work when only the indigenous people lived here. God was at work long before we came.

We need to seek counsel and ask a lot of questions. We need to be open. We need to go to people whom we trust, people whom we give permission to speak truthfully, firmly, and lovingly. We need to ask people to point out our blind spots.

Early on, some people asked me why I felt as though I needed to do this and why I just didn't give my donation to an existing nonprofit. This forced me to wrestle with those questions. I felt by starting ODW I could inspire thousands of people, to engage them in this dream of fighting poverty.

Good storytellers are people who live a good story.

So this one time, when I was in Kenya, I was abducted, and it was super scary.

(No, not really.)

How Jesus Handled It

This may be obvious, but I'll just throw it out there. Both by our standards and those of His culture, Jesus acted strangely.

Jesus did not care about drawing attention to Himself. Think of the moments when He challenged authority, when He cleared the temple, or when He spoke to people whom society had rejected. It's difficult to imagine Him doing these things out of any sort of narcissistic desire.

One of many aspects that amazes me most about Jesus is when He tells people to be quiet about His miracles. "Don't tell anyone," He would say.

It's mind-boggling because it was so countercultural, both then and now, to hide the miraculous.

Check out this passage from Matthew in which Jesus cured two blind men:

> Then he touched their eyes and said, "According to your faith let it be done to you"; and their sight was restored. Jesus warned them sternly, "See that no one knows about this." But they went out and

spread the news about him all over that region.
(Matt. 9:29–31)

If Jesus had an agent to help Him with publicity, this miracle
would've been all over the news. If His disciples were there to witness
it, they would have said, "We have got to make this go viral! We have
got to share this with folks."

There's something about His time in the desert that I also find to
be quite profound: His times of fasting and praying. I'm fascinated by
the idea of Jesus going off to pray and retreat. The Son of God, *seeking
God*. The Son of God actively separating Himself, reflecting and praying to be true to His identity.

Some tried, even the Devil himself, to manipulate or coerce Jesus
into being something He wasn't called to be. And He took time to pray
and examine Himself and His heart.

All too often in our culture today, Christians and churches try so
hard to build their platforms and make news. We're trying so hard to be
spectacular so that we can, apparently, garner attention for the gospel.

Perhaps we need to examine ourselves again. Why are we so
obsessed with building our platforms? Why are we so obsessed with
a spectacular spirituality?

Today the church is tempted by the spectacular, tempted to do
big, miraculous things so people might believe, but Jesus called us to
the insignificant. He compared "our revolution to the mustard seed,
to yeast making its way through dough, slowly infecting this dark
world with love."[7]

Listen: Just do your thing with passion, joy, honor, and humility,
and folks will notice. Actually, even if no one notices, be faithful

to what God has called you. Remember, we do what we do not for people's applause but for God's glory.

Don't be held captive to either praise or criticism. Know who you are, what you're about, and most important, who you serve.

Check Yourself Before You Wreck Yourself

This is an everyday rhythm. Daily, I ask myself these questions:

> Who am I?
> Whom do I serve?
> What are my values?
> Where am I going?

These questions help me find clarity about *how I will get there.* How I will do it.

Who am I? I am a husband, father, pastor, activist, and humanitarian, but most of all, I am created in the image of God. I am a son of God, broken, received, forgiven.

Who do I serve? I serve Jesus. He is my Lord, my Savior, my anchor. He informs and transforms everything I do.

What are my values? I want to love mercy. Seek justice. I want to walk humbly. I want to be a person who points people to Christ. I want to compel and fascinate people to Christ.

Where am I going? I want to engage the city. I want to engage the public sphere. I want to love well. I want to serve well. I want to teach well. I want to be about those things. I want to be about the widows. I want to be about the orphans. I want to be about the forgotten. I want to be about the poor. I want to be about the marginalized. I want to be about the trafficked. I want to be about these things because I believe these are near the heart of God.

This is who I am. This is what I'm about. All those things inform how I want to live my life. I feel called to the things that I truly care about, and these are the things that God has wired me to do. There are days, moments, stretches where I feel battered and beaten. I feel exhausted. I hear the criticism. The more you seek to do good work, the more you will get your share of criticism.

The answers to those questions about who I am, whom I serve, why I do what I do, and what I am about keep me connected to my calling.

So as I'm fishing, driving across the country with nothing but time, or walking around my neighborhood, I think about these things. I invite Minhee and those I love to ask me the hard questions in that place.

For me—and I pray for you as well—may these questions and our times of prayer and reflection serve as our anchors. Amen.

Chapter 7

HAVING MORE DEPTH THAN 140 CHARACTERS: BE AN EXPERT

I stepped onto the stage, walked to the podium, and looked across the crowd of several hundred college students.

"Hey, everyone," I said. "Great to be here. My name is Eugene Cho, and I'd like to begin tonight by having you open your Bibles and turn to the book of Shaquille, chapter 13, verses 1–14."

About half of the young men and women at the Christian college retreat in Southern California flipped open their Bibles and began looking. I heard the rustling of pages, seeing many students hunched over their Bibles. I am sure there were a few people in the crowd smirking.

But so many students kept looking … *and looking*.

When they didn't find the book of Shaquille by thumbing through their Bibles, they flipped to the table of contents. And scanned. They discreetly whispered to one another, asking for help. Of course, we don't want others to know we can't find the book of Shaquille.

I wasn't trying to be cruel, but I let this social experiment go on for a few minutes—long enough for it to become awkward. I wanted people to look.

Eventually, I broke the news.

"Hey, folks," I said. "I'm not here to make fun of people or shame anyone. The truth is, there is no book of Shaquille. My sermon today is about our lack of depth, knowledge, and commitment. If something matters to us, we need to know it. We need to learn it. We need to commit to studying. We need to commit to going deep."

I remember seeing some shocked faces, and then the students started laughing nervously.

I may or may not have been a jerk that night. I didn't intend to be a jerk, but I wanted to lay it out there for the students: I am quite concerned about our collective lack of depth. I'm speaking to them. I'm speaking to myself. And yes, I'm speaking to you.

I believe that while humans are getting smarter on the whole and we have access to information as never before, in some ways, we might be getting shallower as well. Before you throw a stone my way, hear what I'm trying to say:

This chapter (again) is—more than anything—a confession.

We lean on our smartphones and the Internet for so much information. We haven't taken the time to study and digest the things we read. We are a fast-food culture. We hate chewing on data and information and internalizing it. It is not personal to us. So often, we're content to skim the surface.

I want to affirm God's goodness. God's call upon my life and yours. I want to affirm our convictions. That's the easy part.

The hard part is owning it and forming something deeper in our lives, with God's grace. The hard part is answering the call to justice. Answering the call to research and learn and know. Answering the call to discipleship.

Simply put: We must dig deep.

Hello, #Hashtag Generation! #Holla!

I would contend that the culture today is light on wisdom and lacking a depth of substantive understanding. Our limited attention span spreads our affections thin, yielding shallow roots.

Agree or disagree?

We live in a social-media world, and you know what that means: Social media–minded people think in status updates and hashtags. #BestChapterEver

They think in tweets. #Cho-tastic

They compress ideas into 140 characters or less. #EducateYourself

They like videos, but short ones. In fact, six-second videos are long enough. Fifteen-second videos might be a stretch. Hashtags, anyone?

If we are not careful, these snapshots of information and entertainment can trick us into believing we actually know something, or worse, that we're actually doing something. #awesome

I get it. Facebook. Twitter. Tumblr. YouTube. Blogging. Social media and new media are all part of our fast-changing cultural landscape. I get it because I use social media. Not only are they important tools for our culture, but they are actually part of the language we speak in our current context. I speak this language. It has value and is important, but we have to make sure that these tools don't encapsulate the totality of our knowledge, engagement, and action.

Want some examples?

I've had conversations with hundreds of people who are passionate but unfortunately haven't taken the time to go deep in their area of passion or conviction. And thus these conversations are painfully short. Listen, if something matters to you, *then go deep*. Take the time, and make a commitment to be an expert in the areas of your passion. Don't just say that you saw it on *Wikipedia* or heard it on NPR or read someone's Facebook status.

I'm not suggesting that everyone who has a particular calling, passion, or conviction has to go back to school. I am not suggesting that we must earn a doctorate in a particular field, but we do have to commit to learning, studying, and becoming critical thinkers. My hope for you, as it is for me, is that we can have the ability to be thoughtful, prayerful, critical, and knowledgeable in order that we might engage the larger marketplace of ideas and make things happen.

If something matters to you, then study it. Learn it. Engage it. Go deep in it.

#GottaGoDeeper #GottaBeDeeper

Tweet that.

But, I Don't Have Time for Depth ...

Yes, you do.

We need to be honest with ourselves. Sometimes the words "too busy" are substitutes for "too lazy." At least that's true for me. What about you?

An argument we often use with ourselves is that we don't have enough time to go deep, to really know the intricacies of something that we care about. While you and I might lead busy lives, we still find time for what we truly care about.

Earlier in this book I mentioned my obsession with convertible cars. Confession time: I also have a thing for RVs. A few years ago I got absolutely infatuated with RVs. I didn't have one, but I knew more about them than any sane person should.

I had stacks of brochures about RVs. Nearly every single night, before I went to bed, I would look through these brochures, imagining how great it would be to have my own RV. I studied the specs, details, dimensions, gas mileage, and amenities. I tried to determine which one might be best for me someday when this book hits the *New York Times* bestsellers list. Just kidding.

There was a family in our church who owned an older RV, and they were generous to allow my family to use it for a couple of nights.

"You probably don't know much about RVs, so let us explain it to you," the owner began when he brought it over.

I interjected, "So, this is a Winnebago Rialta, right?"

"Yup." He was pleasantly surprised.

"And by looking at the dimensions and amenities, this appears to be a 22FD."

They were absolutely shocked. Awkwardly surprised. It was, of course, a model 22FD.

When I think about the amount of time I have obsessed about RVs, I know that "too busy" is not an honest reflection of my time.

If something matters to us, we must invest in it. We must commit to going deeper. Our time here on this planet is finite. We have to choose to invest and go deep on things that matter to us.

Know History, Know Respect, Know Context

I am the first to tell you that I don't know everything about everything. But when it comes to my core pursuits, my passions, the issues that inspire me and drive me to serve, I try to learn as much as I can.

Over the past few years, I have met many people who are not only interested in serving the world in various ways but who are engaged in their convictions and passions. But I am often surprised to find out that they do not know the basic history and background of their chosen interest.

I remember one time in particular, at a conference, when a woman came up to me and told me she was very grateful and appreciative of a talk I had just given. We chitchatted, and eventually I asked her what she did as her vocation.

She said she worked at an NGO, serving the poor in Central America. We were having a polite conversation. She asked for advice, and I tried my best to encourage her in our short conversation. As I shared one of my favorite quotes from Óscar Romero, I asked her if she had read much of his works or about him.

She had this blank look on her face.

"No, I haven't met him yet, but I'd love to. Can you connect me? How can I contact him?"

An awkward silence ensued.

It dawned on me at that point that she had never heard about Archbishop Romero—who, by the way, was assassinated on March 24, 1980.

"I'm sorry. Please don't take this the wrong way. I really want to encourage you. You're doing some great work in your communities, so be encouraged. As you keep doing deep work in your community and because you feel led to serve the larger communities throughout Central America, you need to understand the history of Central America. The equivalent of you not knowing about Óscar Romero in your context is if you were to say that you care about civil rights in America and not know about Martin Luther King Jr."

Another awkward silence.

Please don't judge me. It sounded much more pastoral and kind when I said it. Really! I gave her a huge hug and encouraged her to keep pressing on, going deeper, caring well, leading well, listening well, and loving well.

You may or may not know about Óscar Romero, but I hope you learn about him, especially if you ever choose to serve the poor in Latin America. Romero spoke out against poverty, social injustice, assassinations, and torture.[1] He was an outspoken advocate for the poor and vulnerable as security crumbled in El Salvador in the late 1970s.[2]

He was celebrating mass at a hospital, lifting a chalice during the sacrament, when he was shot.

The assassination sparked an international uproar, coming one day after he preached a sermon that implored soldiers to act like Christians and stop carrying out the government's ongoing repression.

Óscar Romero has an important story to be heard. And there are many others, if you take the time to dig in and learn. To better understand issues of poverty, justice, and classism in Latin America, how can one not take the time to study and learn from theologians such as Dominican priest Gustavo Gutiérrez and the Jesuit priest Juan Luis Segundo?

How can we say we care about abolition and not know the story of William Wilberforce?

How can we say we care about the history of slavery and abolitionism in the United States and not know about Harriet Tubman or Frederick Douglass or Harriet Beecher Stowe or William Lloyd Garrison?

How can we say we care about women's equality in America and not know the likes of Susan B. Anthony (who also taught at a seminary), Elizabeth Cady Stanton, and Sojourner Truth?

How can we say we care about the civil rights movement and racial justice and not know the story of Emmett Till?

How can we say we care about Asian American context or ministry and not know the story of Vincent Chin?[3]

Okay. I'm just gonna lay it down because, as an Asian American myself, I'd love for all readers to at least have an understanding of why Vincent Chin is important to Asian American history.

Chin was a Chinese American man, beaten to death in 1982 by Ronald Ebens—the superintendent of a Chrysler plant—and his nephew. Chin's murder in Detroit sparked an uprising.

The superintendent shouted at him, "It's because of [people like you] that we're out of work!" referring to US auto-manufacturing jobs being lost to Japan. Of course, Chin wasn't even Japanese.

The two attackers tracked him down to a McDonald's, after they initially encountered Chin at his bachelor party. It was there that the nephew held him and Ebens severely bludgeoned him with a baseball bat. Days later, Chin died.

Initially, Ebens and his nephew were sentenced to no prison time for the brutal, apparently racially motivated murder. It was a catalyst to open the dialogue about racially motivated hate crimes, the marginalization of immigrants, and the injustice of unfair criminal sentencing.

Point being, you can't know everything about everything, but when you say that you care about something in particular, and feel called about it, this is where I say you have to dig deep, be deep. Take time to understand the issues, facts, complexities, and nuances. Without knowing even the basic background of what you care about, you can hurt the people you are trying to help. This is an issue of respect.

All issues have their form in a community of history, context, and culture. If we miss these things, we simply are not doing our jobs well. We're not caring well, listening well, and not setting up ourselves well for mutual relationship.

Never stop learning. Study the Bible. Read the news. Devour books. Engage people. Ask questions. Be a critical thinker and active practitioner.

Your move.

Going Deep: Local Homelessness

Once I learn more about an issue, I realize everything's not as black and white as I had imagined. For example, I think about the complexities of homelessness. *Homeless* is a very broad word.

When we look at the 2,500-plus people in the Seattle area[4]—on any given night—who are homeless *and* living on the streets, it's heartbreaking. Let's be honest. If we look at these homeless people, we often make or have sweeping assumptions and generalizations, and they're often not good ones.

Don't be lazy and make assumptions about people. Ask about their stories. Then, listen. Really listen. Be humble. Be teachable. Be human. Not just of the poor. Not just of the homeless but of all people.

The typical assumptions we have of homeless people are that they are bums and they're lazy. And that most of them can't get jobs because they don't want jobs. From my discussions with men and women without homes, going without a job is often not for a lack of trying. Certainly, addictions and mental instability play big roles as well. As a pastor, neighbor, and one of the instigators behind the Bridge Care Center—Quest Church's homeless advocacy ministry— I have had many conversations with people enduring homelessness.

Consider some of these statistics that convey the complexities of being homeless:

- Wage earners must make $12.29 an hour for forty hours a week to afford the average one-bedroom apartment in King County.
- Between 1993 and 1995, the number of units affordable to low-income renters dropped by nine hundred thousand units nationwide.
- In 315 of 399 US metropolitan areas, 40 percent or more of renters cannot afford the fair market rent for a two-bedroom unit.

- Minimum-wage workers cannot afford a two-bedroom apartment anywhere in the United States.
- In 1998, applicants waited an average of twenty-eight months for a Section 8 rental assistance voucher.[5]

As a college student, I double majored in psychology and theater. I was never able to complete my degree in theater because I chose to graduate college early and, more truthfully, I sucked as an actor. I was cast for two measly productions, and in one of them, I was playing a homeless person. The director called me into his office one day to bluntly explain to me that I simply did not understand my character, and he challenged me to spend a few days out in the streets as a homeless person. So, I did. I trekked to downtown San Francisco and assumed the role, at least in my mind, dressing in my worst clothes and wrapping myself in a sleeping bag. I sat outside a Macy's store on Market Street with a cardboard sign, panhandling for money. In a few days, I saw thousands of people walk by me. A few gave me their spare change.

Emotionally, this experience became far more than research for a role. What happened really broke me: Thousands of people walked past me, as I mentioned, but *not a single person* looked me in the eye.

It was the most demeaning, degrading, undignified feeling I have ever experienced. In short, I felt invisible.

When you talk about the issue of homelessness, you might just think of it as an issue. But what we need to understand is that there is a real human being, a human soul, a man or woman or even a child—just like you and me—behind the issue. We need to be "people who are building deep, genuine relationships with fellow strugglers along the way, and who actually know the faces of the people behind the issues they are concerned about."[6]

If we really care about the issue of homelessness, we need to recognize the individual whom God has created. We need to recognize his or her humanity. But if we really care about justice, if we care about the individuals who have fallen on hard times, we must do more than give a smile or a handout.

We need to understand the social issues. The policy issues. What affordable housing looks like. Why there is a lack of beds on a given night. What resources are available.

We need to be able to advocate wisely, to our friends, our church, and our elected officials. We need to have learned enough, be engaged enough, committed enough to that process so that when we are speaking to people, we can speak in layman's language. When we speak with elected officials, we need to engage in critical thought and be able to talk about policy. When we talk with our pastors, theologians, and those in the church, we need to be able to engage with theology and scriptures.

Going Deep: Global Water Solutions

It's easy to look for the simple solutions. One area where I have seen this again and again is in regard to water—particularly because water (like human trafficking) tends to be a popular issue for people today. One can say that these issues have gone mainstream.

But nevertheless, the reality is that we still have a water crisis. One in nine people alive today do not have access to clean water, and with that comes a cost to productivity, widespread disease, and even death. Every day three thousand children under age five die needlessly because of waterborne disease.[7]

Do you remember the early video game *The Oregon Trail*? In the game, played in glamorous low-resolution green-and-black graphics, the player guided settlers across the native lands we now call America. Heading west, the group encountered a variety of obstacles and often became sick and even died from diseases we've cured in the Western world, such as cholera, typhoid, or dysentery.

While it might have been a game we enjoyed in the early eighties on newfangled Apple IIs, the diseases the player "encountered" are not a game to millions of people in the developing world, even today. The fact is, people still die from these horrible diseases, often transmitted because of contaminated water.

The cause of death from these diseases is usually dehydration. Severe diarrhea causes water depletion from the body, and in some cases, if too much water is lost, the sufferer will die.

And a disease such as cholera, which is painful and humiliating, can kill within hours if left untreated.[8]

So what is the solution to the water crisis? Dig more water wells?

True story. I can't count the number of conversations I've had with people who were convicted, had epiphanies, callings, revelations … about the water crisis, and desperately wanted to build water wells because that's what they saw on television. They suddenly feel the urge to build water wells in Africa or Asia or some other apparently random country. They then want to spend several thousand dollars to travel to take pictures of that water well with many smiling children drenching themselves with clean water.

"Anywhere. I just want to build a water well," said one person I met a couple of years ago.

"Why?"

"Because there's a water crisis and people don't have access to clean water. I feel called to do something, and I want to build a water well."

"Okay. Why water wells? Is that the best solution? Actually, tell me some of the other solutions that you've researched."

There was an awkward silence for a few moments.

While there are few things in development as spectacular as seeing water gush out of the ground after a well is drilled, what happens in year two, five, and ten is far more important, and difficult. By many reports, more than one-third of all wells drilled in the last twenty years are now broken—fifty thousand are currently broken in Africa alone, preventing access to clean water for millions of people. Some experts say as many as 60 percent of wells in the developing world aren't working.[9] Wells often break within a few years, and in most instances, there are no trained mechanics, spare parts, or tools nearby … or the local community is not invested enough to maintain the well.

That's why good community development must work with communities to equip people to care for their water systems, long after the "grand opening" ribbon-cutting ceremonies have faded from memory. If some organization comes in, drills wells, and doesn't teach people the importance of clean water or teach how to care for the systems from a community level, it's a disservice to the community.

And wells are not the only solution for access to clean water.

In certain areas of the world, you simply cannot dig wells. The water table is too low to be reasonably accessed, or the groundwater is too saline. In these places your best bet may be to create rain-catchment systems. These systems collect rain through gutters installed on the roofs of community buildings or schoolhouses, or collect rainwater in the form of platforms on the ground, which guide water into protected underground chambers.

Granted, this is not as glamorous as digging a well. It's always fun to see water shoot up from the ground. But these alternative systems can be even *more* effective, and that's what we're after, right? Not good promotional pictures and selfies, right? One of these rain-catchment systems can provide water to a community for several months, even after only a single storm passes by. In northern Somalia, these systems, called *berkads*, catch seventy thousand gallons of rainwater and are the only good way to collect suitable drinking water, providing a lifeline to hundreds of people.[10]

And wells and rain-catchment systems alone are not the solution either. Bio-sand filters—an innovative version of the slow sand filter—are quickly garnering attention as very affordable, simple, and effective in providing clean water to households.

Clean-water initiatives must come in tandem with sanitation and education. Sure, one in nine humans do not have access to safe drinking water. But consider nearly four in ten do not have access to toilets, according to the UN. That's 37 percent of your fellow humans without a decent place to go to the bathroom.[11]

Imagine that. Not having access to a toilet. And imagine how disease spreads without proper sanitation. No wonder those *Oregon Trail* diseases continue to kill.

WASH is a term used by those in the humanitarian world to encompass the whole solution: Water, Sanitation and Hygiene.[12] It all has to come together. Throw in that respective community engagement to the ideas behind why people need to wash hands, use toilets, and maintain wells, and you might have a chance to have a significant and even lasting impact.

One Day's Wages has also partnered with NGOs, such as Well Done Liberia, that have conducted hygiene and sanitation training for members of their communities using Participatory Hygiene and Sanitation Transformation (PHAST) methods. Members are taught about disease transmission, routes and methods to block them, and how health is linked to water and sanitation. Hygiene programs such as PHAST have been proven to reduce waterborne diseases by upward of 45 percent.

My point?

It's not just about the feel-good image of one particular solution. In this case, the water well. With the crisis of access to clean water, a water well is just one option, and when implemented, it must always go hand in hand with education and training.

A Final Reminder

The work of justice is not only long and laborious, but it also needs to have depth. The invitation of discipleship is not just a marathon; it is an invitation to costly discipleship.

We owe it to ourselves to be prayerful, knowledgeable, and committed to being experts on the work and conviction to which we feel called. While we may never fully get there, it's a lifelong commitment to be a learner. This is, in essence, what it means to be a disciple.

So, let me close this chapter with two questions for you to ponder:

What are you passionate about?

How are you going deep?

Chapter 8

DON'T ASK OTHERS TO DO WHAT YOU'RE NOT WILLING TO DO YOURSELF

Although we have received a lot of praise for starting One Day's Wages, we also received a lot of criticism and skepticism, especially at the beginning. And some of the criticism was convicting.

The main critique lobbed against me in particular was that we should not give publicly, but only give privately. Many people quoted Scripture to me, which in itself is always hard to respond to, especially if they're quoting Jesus preaching the Sermon on the Mount:

> So when you give to the needy, do not announce it with trumpets, as the hypocrites do in the synagogues and on the streets, to be honored by others. Truly I tell you, they have received their reward in

full. But when you give to the needy, do not let
your left hand know what your right hand is doing,
so that your giving may be in secret. Then your
Father, who sees what is done in secret, will reward
you. (Matt. 6:2–4)

Minhee and I spent much time wrestling with this decision. We
knew we would get our share of criticism, and ultimately we had
peace with the decision to go public with our pledge. Our motivation in this decision wasn't to appear altruistic or to receive pats on
our backs, but rather we felt it was important to speak directly to a
growing cynicism in our world today of people who were weary of
people talking the good talk but not necessarily walking the walk.

I was reminded of these simple and profound words from St.
Francis of Assisi: "It is no use walking anywhere to preach unless our
walking is our preaching."

Not that we were trying to debate or argue with our critics, but
we also found conviction and encouragement from the words of
Jesus in Matthew 5:16:

In the same way, let your light shine before others,
that they may see your good deeds and glorify your
Father in heaven.

We believed it was important to honor one of our life convictions: Don't ask people to do what you're not willing to do yourself.
In other words:

Don't ask people to pray if you're not willing to pray.

Don't ask people to fast if you're not fasting.

Don't ask people to serve if you're not willing to serve.

Don't ask people to live sacrificially if you're not willing to live sacrificially.

Don't ask people to volunteer if you're not willing to volunteer.

In starting the vision of One Day's Wages, we felt we needed to demonstrate our commitment. In giving a year of our wages, we wanted to ask people to join the cause by simply donating one *day's* wages.

Why Would You Do That?

People often ask me, "How did One Day's Wages blow up? How is it able to do what it's doing? What's your formula? Who did you work with for marketing and branding?"

They ask technical questions. Essentially, they are asking, "How did you do it, so that I can replicate it?"

First of all, nothing has blown up. We are a very small grassroots organization. For the first two years of our organization, we had only one full-time employee. I can now proudly say we've grown our staff by 100 percent, from one to two full-time employees. Our team is made up of interns, volunteers, and several board members who have sacrificially invested in ODW. We have no marketing team or branding team. We don't even currently have a graphic artist. We get help from those who are able to help—from season to season.

Yes, we created a website, and we spent much time on it to make it look as sharp and as innovative as we could. We also worked hard to present our message with clarity.

We did ask a friend to help us with our logo.

We did create a video.

We did start social-media accounts.

We did contact the media.

All of this was done largely with a one-person volunteer team (me) being supported by a loving and understanding family. Once we launched, I hired my first employee and paid her what we could ($28,000 as a full-time salary).

We worked out of our basement for a while. Then rented a very small office. Maybe three hundred square feet. *Maybe.* I can talk about all these different elements, but it isn't really why we've been blessed with "success," I believe.

What brought all of this together, what kept One Day's Wages in the spotlight, was the story. Our family's story. I believe it was our family's decision to not just like the idea of doing something, but to actually do something.

People were fascinated: leaders, institutions, media, and the general public. The most common question we fielded again and again was, "Why would you do that?"

Questions of genuine interest continued: "Why would a family with three young children give up a year's wages?" "Why would a family go couch surfing to raise money for the poorest of the poor?"

The reason why ODW managed to resonate with the public was not because of slick branding or marketing. We gained momentum because our story resonated with and inspired people, because ultimately, actions speak louder than any branding or messaging we could have developed.

We are not millionaires. We are not rock stars. We are not celebrities. We are just an average family trying to pursue our convictions. We're just an average family trying to live lives of faith, hope, and love.

We shared our story because we wanted to inspire people. We wanted people to join us, so that it was not just us. That was part of our conviction, to make it not just us, but God working through us. We wanted to be a conduit, so that God could work through many.

What a joy and privilege it has been to be able to speak to so many people—including and especially non-Christians who have asked about our motivation—and to speak genuinely about our faith in Christ and how that has compelled us to not just tell a better story but to live a better story.

Live What You Speak

I admire the apostle Paul, in part because he had a life-changing transformation. But it didn't stop there. He didn't allow it to be the only transformative event of his life.

Paul chose to actively live out the gospel, and with that came a huge personal cost. He believed so deeply in Jesus's call to tell the world about salvation that he gave up his life for the cause.

Paul persevered …

… even when religious leaders and the nonreligious rejected him;

… even when he was criticized; and

… even when he spent a year traveling from city to city, with no family, no home.

To see him being steadfast inspires me. The gospel he professed inspires me. He lived deep into the gospel, and through that deep investment, we saw the Word come alive. We see people like this in the present day.

Although I'm not Catholic, I've got to tell you the new pope is dope. I see Catholicism as a part of Christianity, but I've not been a huge fan of popes before. There are things about Catholicism that I have criticized, and there are in fact easy criticisms to make. The money. The power. The controversies. The sexual scandals. These are painful things.

The example of Pope Francis has been refreshing. He took a vow of poverty early in his ministry and has never gone back. Since he has been elevated to the papacy, the former Jorge Mario Bergoglio has elected to live in the papal guesthouse, not the four-star accommodations where previous popes lived.[1] He wants people to know that he is with them, not above them. He likes the idea of being in community and close to others, rather than on his own, living in luxury.

Quite frankly, Catholics and the general public have been shocked. They can't believe his humility and the way he lives out the gospel. As far as I'm concerned, this should not be a big deal.

As the leader of the church, *every* pope should act like this. Pope Francis's actions are consistent with what we read about in Scripture. It shouldn't be earth-shattering or surprising, and yet the new pope's behavior is entirely countercultural. His story—early on—washing feet and welcoming dialogue with laypeople shows his heart and, most important, reflects the heart of Christ.

People are amazed by his example, because in our world today, people are cynical about religion and religious leaders. Most believe that religious leaders teach in word only, not in deed.

People also see the fallacy of the prosperity gospel. Anyone who finds him- or herself immersed in consumer culture can tell you that you will never satisfy your desire for things. You will always want more. It's been proven time and again, even with kids,[2] that satisfaction comes not from accumulating stuff but from giving rather than receiving.[3] And yet, the gospel preached in commercials and in popular culture is that of accumulation and luxury.

Have you heard about that Nigerian pastor—Bishop David Oyedepo—who owns four private planes? Reportedly, he was recently bent out of shape because he had to sell a couple of them.[4] And he's not alone. There are at least two other Nigerian pastors with multimillion-dollar private jets, in a country where most people live in poverty or extreme poverty.[5] What do their stories reflect?

Unfortunately, we don't have to look that far for other examples. We can look in the United States and share a list of pastors and religious leaders who flaunt their opulent lifestyles, which include city penthouses, numerous extravagant vacation homes, and private jets. With leaders like these, I can't blame people for being cynical about religion.

I'm not saying we have to pledge lives of poverty, but there's something about living simply and generously that connects with the heart of God. It testifies to God's blessedness in our lives, and it speaks to people about the fact that God is alive and well, working through people today.

I think of my family. We have clothes, food. We are able to eat what we want to eat. We have a beautiful home. So in terms of physical needs, we have everything we need. I think about the blessing and richness of relationships and community and the family that loves us and supports us.

Some days I feel that I am the richest man in the world. On the other days, I wrestle with the tension of upward mobility and need to be reminded how blessed I am.

We try, and succeed. We try, and fail.

In it all, I hope and pray that our direction is consistent. I hope and pray that our life testifies to our faith in God and our generosity to others.

We cannot speak with integrity about what we are not living. We don't need more dazzling storytellers; we need more genuine storytellers. And the best way to become a better storyteller is to simply live a better life. Not a perfect life, but one of honesty, integrity, and passion.

If you believe it, then live it. For it is through our living that we bring credibility to our beliefs.

Actions Speak: The Shaved Head

Meet Anji.

Anji is a married, thirty-eight-year-old mother of four young children, ages ten, eight, four, and one. Her youngest two children were adopted from Ethiopia. Her family resides in the greater Chicago area, and she volunteers for Compassion International, a large humanitarian organization.

One morning as she was washing her hair, she confessed to having several strange thoughts come to her mind:

1. I lose an unbelievable amount of hair when I wash it. Handfuls of hair every time!

2. The weird thing is that I still have a TON of hair left. You'd never know any was missing.

3. Maybe generosity is like that. Maybe generosity should be measured not in terms of how much we give, but in terms of how much we keep.

4. I need to shave my head as a fund-raiser for the famine relief efforts.

5. That's insane. Did I just think that?

She took some time to pray, and I love her story of what happened next:

And so, after a couple of days of wrestling with God, here I am with this challenge to you. In all my life, I have never given sacrificially, because no matter how much I give, I still have enough. More than enough, actually. In this case though, I am going to make a sacrifice. On November 2nd I am going to shave my head. Please help me make it count.[6]

But for what?

She was moved by the drought and famine in eastern Africa—the worst of its kind in that region in the past fifty years, impacting approximately 13.5 million people. This is what she had to say:

I feel other people's pain deeply, which is both a blessing and curse. The ugly truth is that I've spent

weeks purposely avoiding any media about the
famine. While I knew the enormity of the brew-
ing disaster, I managed to keep it at arm's length.
There are 12 million people on the brink of starva-
tion, 1000 refugees per day pouring into already
over-crowded refugee camps, and 29,000 children
dead—and I closed my eyes to it ... kept my world
small.

But all that changed because of a photo-
graph I stumbled across on the internet. Maybe
you've seen it? The wide eyes of a two year old
malnourished child, holding on to the edges of a
wash basin, his skin literally hanging from his tiny
bones. My heart went straight into my throat as it
struck me; that could be my son. That is *someone's*
son.[7]

And so she invited her family and friends to learn about the
situation in the Horn of Africa. She explained why she was choosing
to shave her head, and invited people to make a contribution of any
size. And people gave. And gave. Her friends. Family. Neighbors.
Kids from local schools. The local media picked up her story. Others
were inspired and started their own campaigns.

In choosing to respond to the convictions God had placed upon
her heart, Anji raised $18,175.97, and all of it went to help impact
lives. And she continues to advocate for the poorest of the poor
around the world.

Actions speak louder. Thank you, Anji.

Actions Speak: Churches Serving Local Schools

Education matters. Every school has its challenges, and if we're honest, some schools have more than others. Midway Elementary is a school in an urban neighborhood in Des Moines, Washington—a community south of Seattle. The school has a diverse student population, which contributes to the challenges they face. With more than 90 percent of their student population qualifying as "low income," along with a high immigrant demographic, the school seeks to do more than just teach. The staff use their vision of serving the whole child to increase access to opportunities those children may not otherwise enjoy, especially in comparison to their white middle-class peers in the United States.

Teachers and administrators were doing their best, but what a gift when local churches came without any suspicious agenda, simply asking, "How can we serve you?"

Beautiful, right?

Churches, including Midway Community Covenant Church, Brooklake Church, Highline Seventh-day Adventist, and South-minster Presbyterian Church, collaborated and helped form "Team Midway" with the school.

The vision of Team Midway: "Our purpose is to collaborate with community to support and encourage Midway staff, students, and families in the educational experience, to prepare each child for lifelong learning."

Here's a glimpse of what these churches have been doing to put into action their vision of being good neighbors and serving their local school: They have held literacy events, providing school families with meals, warm coats, and hygiene packs. Volunteers have also regularly participated in back-to-school events, equipping school families with free backpacks, school supplies, haircuts, and everyday necessities to help make the back-to-school transition a positive experience.

In addition, they have worked to increase the educational experience in all realms, including the arts. Midway Community Covenant Church, for example, partnered with staff to create an after-school art program that provided weekly lessons for up to fifty students per quarter. Their collaboration brought state standards–based art instruction to Midway's students, who proudly displayed their artwork in the school building and was featured during the church's annual talent show. Midway Elementary's staff have also benefitted from the partnership with Team Midway by receiving annual staff-appreciation gifts. These tokens of gratitude have included special messages and treats honoring these teachers for what they do for their students.

Beautiful, right?

I asked the principal of Midway Elementary, Rebekah Kim (also a follower of Christ), about Team Midway, and she shared these powerful words in an email:

The love and commitment our local churches have provided for our school community have helped my own personal faith to grow. It is undeniable that God's blessings continue to be poured onto our school. As the principal of this school, I am personally moved by the hands of God being used to bless our children. This is what I call "church," more so than sitting and listening to sermons and walking away without action.

Actions Speak: The Youth Pastor

Meet Joon. Crazy things happen when we yield to God's desire to act justly. And by crazy, I also mean … crazy discomfort. Don't say that I didn't warn you!

In 2012, I received an email from Joon Park, a youth pastor for New Light Church in Tampa, Florida. I'd never met him and had never heard of him. Joon describes himself as "a former atheist/ agnostic, fifth degree black belt, recovered porn addict, and pastor." He said, "Like every other dude with a laptop, I blog regularly. I can eat five lbs. of steak in one sitting. I have a German shepherd named Rosco."[8]

After hearing a talk I gave at the 2011 Catalyst Conference, Joon shared that he was convicted by the Holy Spirit and was now acting upon that conviction. This young youth pastor had decided to donate half of his yearly salary to charity.

Read his email:

Hello Pastor Eugene!

My name is Joon Park. I'm currently a youth pastor of New Light Church in Tampa, Florida.

After a friend of mine sent me your Catalyst Lab from 2011, I was convicted to donate half my salary this year to a charity. That would amount to $10,000, which I understand is not large by certain standards, yet hopefully enough to save a handful of lives. I listened to *your sermon in the car, then at Sweet Tomatoes (where I felt sick over the affluence of a culture that needs buffets), and by the time I got home, with tear-drenched eyes I knew what I had to do.*

I wanted to personally thank you for your message. I checked out your websites, and I believe in what the Holy Spirit is doing in your life. Though I haven't decided where I will donate the money yet, I am seriously considering your One Day's Wages program.

I am a "nobody" pastor with a 30+ youth group and a blog like every other pastor … Please pray that I may stay encouraged and faithful to my pledge. I'm pretty scared. You are right. We cannot ask of others what we don't do ourselves.

Wow. How crazy, radical, and countercultural is this?

Think about it: Young. Youth pastor. Donating half of his salary = $10,000. #convicting

Wouldn't you know it, Joon asked his community to step up in various ways, and opportunities opened up for him to take on extra work or receive extra income. He felt blessed *to get* to give.

I have often told people that generosity isn't merely for the sake of blessing others. God calls us to be generous, because in giving to others, we are blessed. Our generosity blesses others, certainly, but it also rescues us from the idolatry of greed in our own lives.

The inescapable truth about justice is that there is something wrong that needs to be set right. Sometimes the things that need to be set right are not in the lives of those we seek to serve. The things that need to be set right are in our own lives.

We need to pursue justice not just because the world is broken, but because we are. Pursuing justice helps us put our own lives in order.

Here's the kicker to Joon's story: He invited friends and family to check out his campaign page on ODW's website and extended a friendly challenge to "match" his donation. Friends, family, and his youth group students did what they could and raised $1,915. Months passed and a random person stumbled across his story on my blog, was moved and convicted, and made an anonymous donation of $8,085, thus helping Joon raise a total of $20,000—all of which went toward fighting human trafficking.

Actions speak louder. Thank you, Joon.

Actions Speak: The Sixteen-Year-Old High School Student

Meet Wylie. He's a sixteen-year-old high school student. In the summer of 2012, Wylie bicycled more than 3,200 miles from Savannah, Georgia, to Los Angeles, California.

This is Wylie's story:

> No, Wylie isn't a super-athlete or a hardcore cyclist. He hasn't done an Ironman Triathlon or run a full marathon. There isn't anything especially distinct about him, but in a grassroots movement, you don't have to be. He chose a bicycle because it is human powered and travels slowly – running at an average speed of 12 mph. By travelling without luxuries, he seeks to meet new people, share stories, see his country from a new perspective, and above all, connect on a deeper level to everything

around him. The challenge of the water crisis is a long battle far from won and he is simply joining One Day's Wages in the fight.

Objective

By cycling over 3,000 miles across the country, he seeks to inspire himself and others alike to realize that biking is a practical way to commute, a unique method of travel, and an easy way to stay fit.

To raise awareness about the global need for bicycles and their role in poverty alleviation. Using the word global, not international, because now more than ever, bicycles have a role in job creation and community building in the United States too. Bicycles are catalysts in making our world a more equitable and accessible place.

To bring light to the water crisis that affects 800 million – 1 billion people. Make a dent in the issue by funding the building of a well and brining clean, safe drinking water to ~250 people in a community previously without it. Inspire others to donate their birthday and start their own campaigns to turn the tide on the issue. The battle is far from won, but all we can do is join in the fight.[9]

Wylie shared his story and conviction with as many people as possible: his school, church, *The Huffington Post*, and the local media.

And while many thought it would be impossible for him to reach his goal of raising $10,000 for his clean-water campaign, he did it. While many thought he was crazy and unable to cycle 3,200 miles across America, he did it.

Actions speak louder than words. Thank you, Wylie.

People Know Your Heart

It's worth repeating: Don't ask someone to do something you are not willing to do.

You lead by how you live.

There are a lot of books and philosophies about leadership. I'm sure they are all good. I have not read many of them. This is less about leadership and more about how we want to live. We want to incarnate the things that we care about. A life deeply and courageously lived resonates with people. A life of integrity resonates with people.

If people know that you believe it, that you are invested, and they know that you are not just skimming the surface, they will begin to realize that it's not something you're selling. Not something you want to monetize.

They will realize that this work is part of who you are.

This is what speaks to us as we look at other people. When we look at people we admire and appreciate, it's not just the words that they say, their moving oratory skills. It is not their blogging or their tweeting. It's not their platform or tribe.

We admire them because they're living out their lives with integrity. It is the fact that they truly live what they believe. It is imperfect, not a marketing machine or polished brand, but as broken human beings, they are actually fleshing out and living out what they believe.

One of the largest criticisms of Christianity is hypocrisy.

Hypocrisy is the act of preaching one thing and doing another, or promising one thing and not delivering. Christians are known for proclaiming their stance against things they hate or at least disagree with, rather than being "for" anything.

Just think of how differently Christians would be seen, understood, and heard if we realigned our mind-sets, and

... if we recognized that we lead imperfect lives and lived from that humility;

... if our first instinct was to disagree with people less, and love people more; and

... if our imperfect life trajectory at least pointed in the right direction, toward redemption and reconciliation with others.

Actions speak louder than words. The best way to become a better storyteller is to simply live a more honest, deep, and faithful life.

Your move.

Chapter 9

THE IRONY OF DOING JUSTICE ... UNJUSTLY

Get ready. This is a painful chapter. Painful to write, and perhaps painful to read. There's such painful irony when people pursue justice ... unjustly. Please be wise and kind. Don't fabricate. Empower people. Treat people with dignity.

When I talk about doing justice unjustly, it might sound a bit harsh. I mean, really, when we're trying to do good in the world, isn't that enough?

We're all busy.

We all have full lives.

Why can't we just do our best and be satisfied with that?

Why can't we celebrate the good intentions of others rather than critiquing?

Remember what I've been sharing throughout this book: I think it's great that people are interested and engaged in doing justice. Yes, we should celebrate this, but most important is *how* we do justice.

I'm not saying it's necessary to criticize someone's good heart, but we should definitely consider the implications of how we engage in the work of justice.

So we want to collect five hundred thousand pairs of shoes and send them to Africa?

Great idea! I have some old shoes. Where do I send them?

Okay, maybe not the greatest idea. Maybe.

But we have to ask.

Is it what's most needed? Did we ask local leaders and communities? Have we considered shipping costs? How will we disrupt the local ecosystem and marketplace for shoes? Or perhaps, how might it ruin those who sell or fix shoes for a living in that context? I mean, it's really hard to compete with free … in any market. Do we know if it really addresses the core causes of poverty?

So we want to collect canned food every week at the church?

That's good. It does help the poor, at least in the short term. But is there a better way, or are there additional ways? What about equipping those who are struggling to break the cycle of unemployment or underemployment?

I'm simply asking questions:

Is it possible to do justice … unjustly? Is it possible that we're doing justice and creating an unhealthy dependence? Is it possible that we're doing justice and making ourselves out to be Western saviors or heroes? Is it possible that we're doing justice by exploiting the poor and not extending dignity?

I have seen this over and over, when do-gooders are inclined to do what they feel is best. They have an idea, an inspiration, a passion—and they pursue it.

"When doing justice or engaging in charity, good intentions do not guarantee a good outcome," wrote Ken Wytsma in his book, *Pursuing Justice*. "We need to build and develop capacity over time. Most development organizations know and practice this, but there are still too many instances of unintended harm that begin with compassion. We need to be held accountable, like a good shepherd, for the final outcome of our love, compassion, and giving."[1]

Without knowing the nuances.

Without going deep.

Without reflection and prayer.

Without first learning the history of the issue and committing to become an expert.

Without genuine humility.

And, sadly, without asking the people you're trying to help what they think.

I don't want to question somebody's motivation, or the heart behind why he or she wants to act. But having a good heart is not enough. It's not enough when our actions affect the lives of others ... especially people who are already vulnerable.

At times we choose to help others in a way that makes us feel as good as possible. When I say "we," I'm including you and me. Perhaps we help others so that we can have a good experience, get good photos, or tell good stories later. This is not enough.

I heard a story from a development worker apropos to the point that I'm trying to make here. A donor representing a US-based nonprofit agency was visiting a village in Bangladesh, and the development worker from a local NGO helped him distribute pajamas for children. That was the entire purpose of the agency's work: providing pajamas to children.

Huh? Pajamas?

Read on ...

One big problem, however, was that this US donor/visitor did not have enough pajamas and said he needed pictures of more children wearing pajamas. So he proposed dressing up some of the local impoverished kids in pajamas, removing them, and then taking pictures of other kids wearing the same pajamas.

"No, I'm not going to do that," the development worker said. "Once the pajamas go from one child to the other, who owns those pajamas? This is unethical."

The donor left angry and disgruntled, saying that others from different NGOs had done it before. He left with half the pictures that he had wanted.

The American donor was also staying at the nice hotel in town, making constant international calls. Mind you, this was in the early eighties, so constant international calls meant that he ran up a couple of thousand dollars' worth of phone bills. And he left the nonprofit with the bill.

"He cost the local nonprofit more than the items he delivered in the first place," they told me.

All of this is not to mention the relevancy of an NGO focused on pajamas. For a moment, consider the absurdity of delivering pajamas into Bangladesh, especially thirty-plus years ago.

For some context, I spoke with Dr. Meredith Long, who has devoted his life to service as a field-worker and executive at World

Concern, MAP International, World Relief, HEED, and other Christian humanitarian organizations.

"At this time in Bangladesh, a tremendous number of kids were dying of preventable disease," Dr. Long said. "We were focused on the core areas of child survival, such as access to and understanding of immunizations, reproductive health, and family planning. A tremendous number of women died in childbirth, putting both a physical and economic strain on families, meaning women were living very short lives. Nutrition was poor, as many, many children died of diarrhea. Oral rehydration was just being developed," Dr. Long said.

As for the need for pajamas: How did that rank on the list of needs for children?

Understand where I'm going with this?

This is not development, not relationship building, and certainly not moving people toward independence, empowerment, or reciprocity. I believe this mind-set is selfish. With this mind-set, we could very well be robbing people of their dignity.

Dare I say it—I believe, in fact, that this way of thinking is sinful.

Though no one can attain perfection in anything in life, we must not be satisfied by imperfectly helping others. "Giving it our best shot" can do damage to those we seek to serve.

As with the rest of this book, I bring this up not because I am perfect. This is self-reflective. A confession.

Indiana Chones to the Rescue!

Indiana Chones. Get it?

Indiana (Cho)nes.

Okay, it was funnier when it first came to mind.

Oftentimes it's the white or Western face that comes in to save the day. Or in my case, the Western Asian man with the Rico Suave beard that appears to be bold, brave, and dramatic (looking off into the distance for dramatic effect).

In places where well-meaning people have been before, whether domestically or internationally, the people we seek to help can feed into this dynamic as well. They can play into this story. They are the ones to be helped, and they say the right things to make us feel good, and they get stuff.

We can easily play right into this. We play our parts as the saviors or heroes. We are blind to it. We feel good about doing it. But this is simply a transactional experience. This is not about life change. The people we serve aren't transformed or renewed or elevated to a better place in life. And we aren't either.

If anything, both parties may end up more corrupted or cynical than before.

No one wins.

In Brian Fikkert and Steve Corbett's book *When Helping Hurts*, they discuss this issue at length:

> Very central point: *one of the biggest problems in many poverty-alleviation efforts is that their design and implementation exacerbates the poverty of being of the economically rich—their god-complexes—and the poverty of being of the economically poor— their feelings of inferiority and shame. The way that we act toward the economically poor often*

communicates—albeit unintentionally—that we
are superior and they are inferior. In the process we
hurt the poor and ourselves.[2]

This kind of mind-set is a game, a damaging game, and if we
choose to play this game, it will distort our own self-perception and
distort the dignity and identities of those we want to help.

What does this say to people in need about their meaning and
their value in life, if they always see themselves as recipients rather
than participants in shaping better futures for themselves?

What does it say to us if we always think of ourselves as the
people with the answers? Is it really all up to us?

The reality is that none of us are the Messiah.

God has a plan. His name is Jesus.

None of us are the Savior. He is.

He has already done the work.

Our role is to listen, learn, and assist however we can. In the
work that we do, we've got to make sure that we each don't paint
ourselves as the Savior.

As Fikkert and Corbett have pointed out, "The economically
rich often have 'god-complexes,' a subtle and unconscious sense of
superiority."[3]

So Who Is the Hero? A Humanitarian Reminisces

If you've worked in international development, you will have seen
many people who are humbly serving as the hands and feet of

God—veritable angels on earth. On the flip side you've probably also met other people who are acting a bit idiotic.

Dr. Meredith Long, field-worker and executive at various NGOs, as mentioned earlier, is in his midsixties now, about six-foot-three-inches tall, with a full head of white hair. He is also an expert in AIDS and community health, and Meredith looks as scholarly as he actually is. He doesn't pretend to have it all figured out, but he was kind enough to share a couple of stories about people attempting to do good in the world and potentially harming others in the process. One story in particular stood out.

In 1980, Meredith worked for MAP International, overseeing a multisector community-development project in Bangladesh. That meant the project was long-term, working with very poor communities to address a variety of needs, including family health, income production, agriculture, education, and so on. It was the kind of project that may take years to see a result, but has a deep and lasting impact on lives.

Once when Meredith was traveling through Bangkok, he met a woman at a guesthouse whom he remembers clearly to this day. The woman might've been about fifty years old. She was well dressed, confident, and appeared to be quite wealthy.

She sat with Meredith at the communal table over dinner. Within a few moments of conversation, it was clear she fancied herself as an American Mother Teresa. She had been traveling from place to place, having an adventure, and possibly doing some good along the way, almost as if the people she was "helping" were an afterthought.

"She immediately began telling stories about her adventures, and what was clear through everything was that she was at the center of it all," Meredith said. "There was no single theme to what she was doing. She would go to an orphanage, she would go to this, go to that. And whenever she would tell a story, it was not about the people who she met. It was how she was changing their lives in some way. The important aspect was that it was she who was doing it."

We all receive a tremendous amount of satisfaction from this kind of work. I know I do. But there are those who are trying to fill a vacancy in their own lives with adventure or self-congratulatory pride.

Beware the savior or hero complex.

You Phonies!

When I was young, I really resonated with Holden Caulfield, the narrator of J. D. Salinger's novel *The Catcher in the Rye*. For the two people reading this who were not assigned *The Catcher in the Rye* in middle-school English, or for those whose school banned the book, here is a thirty-second recap of the story:

Holden is a smart-aleck prep-school dropout experiencing life in New York for a few days before he is to come home for Christmas break. He has a few days to blow, and the story is about his random adventure. The novel is told through Holden's eyes, and he is quick to call disingenuous people "phonies" and criticize the culture unfolding before him, even as he participates in it.

A recurring theme in the book is Holden's inclination to save people. To save people from pain. To save people from seeing things they shouldn't. To save people from the world.

As he walks the streets of New York City with his little sister Phoebe, he mishears the children's song "Comin' Thro' the Rye." The traditional song goes, "If a body meet a body/Comin' thro' the rye,"[4] but he hears it as "If a body catch a body coming through the rye."

Later, Phoebe asks Holden what he wants to do with his life.

Holden thinks about the song, which he has misheard. He imagines children playing in a rye field, near a cliff, and imagines catching them as they fall off. He imagines himself catching the children. *Catcher in the Rye.*

He wants to save them.

He wants to save the children.

He wants to save the children falling off the cliff.

Something about Holden speaks to me. His desire to save children resonates with me. His desire to save the world resonates with me. If I'm honest, I want to catch children and save the world too. Perhaps, this motivation in itself isn't wrong, but what if my motivation to catch children and save the world has more to do with me rather than the children? What if my motivation is to be at the center of this story?

I wonder if all of us struggle, on some level, with this sort of messianic complex.

When we begin a relationship with people we intend to help, we must recognize the power dynamics at work. Are those we seek to "save" at our mercy? What about the complex and poignant history of colonialism? What about the multibillion-dollar engine of nonprofit organizations?

If we want to help, we must consider the reality that many people have tried and failed before us. Our actions take place within a larger story, and we need to be mindful of that truth.

We must consider the attitude of the "savior to the helpless" we unintentionally may convey just by our race, position, or nationality.

BOBS, TOMS, and Other Well-Meaning Guys

Recently, I saw a commercial on TV that I thought was particularly poignant.

It was for BOBS, the Skechers version of TOMS shoes. Same idea: You buy a pair of forty-dollar-plus canvas shoes, and someone in the developing world also gets a pair of shoes. Here's the tagline of the commercial, read by model, reality TV contestant, and *Dancing with the Stars* cohost Brooke Burke:

"BOBS by Skechers. Look good. Feel good. Do good."[5]

Obviously, this is a shoe commercial. The goal is to sell shoes. But nowhere in the commercial do we even see the children who will benefit. Just beautiful models.

So let's analyze the commercial ...

The first priority is to *look good*. The second priority is for you as the consumer to *feel good*. Then it's almost as if, as a bonus, you get around to *doing good*. This is a pretty common order of priority. More often than not, in our Western culture of trying to be the Savior, looking good and feeling good come first.

Do you have a pair of BOBS or TOMS? Or perhaps two? For those who aren't in the "fashion know," BOBS and TOMS are hipster fashion catnip. They look cool and have an image of "good" about them. But the criticism directed at TOMS (and presumably BOBS as well) in the humanitarian world is that the sometimes-airdropped boxes of shoes disrupt the economies they seek to help, and that they are essentially passing off consumption as charity.[6]

Instead of addressing the problems of poverty and unemployment, TOMS and BOBS are merely treating a symptom and are in fact making the economy worse in countries that already have high unemployment.

From a MercyCorps Global Envision post: "A 2008 study found that clothing donations to Africa was responsible for a 50 percent decline in the region's apparel employment. But if the parents have a job, their kids will always have shoes."[7]

And from an article in the *New York Times*: "Since its founding in 2006, [TOMS] has given more than 2 million pairs of shoes to children living in poverty in more than 51 countries,"[8] and the vast majority of those shoes have been manufactured in China.

TOMS may have received some heavy criticism. Perhaps too heavy. Hipsters seem to get a bad rap. Kids are getting shoes when they didn't have any before, right? But TOMS is a for-profit business, "raking in around $250 million in sales,"[9] and like it or not, it does have an impact on the poor and in shaping attitudes in the Western world and developing world.

TOMS founder Blake Mycoskie has been quite candid about all this in recent years. He says he's not under the delusion that his company is the answer for global poverty but points out that it does make a positive impact. Blake got the idea for TOMS from seeing children without shoes in Argentina.

"I didn't come out thinking, 'Hey we're going to solve the world's problems,'" he said. "We're focused on helping people that needed something that we can provide."[10]

I don't want to overly criticize Blake, but I wish that before he launched TOMS he had given more thought to "how" to help, consulting with some experts in development. If the strategy were altered, I believe TOMS would be more universally celebrated.

TOMS continues to evolve, which is encouraging. It is now manufacturing some of its shoes in Ethiopia, in one of the communities that receives the shoes. Similar manufacturing plans are in the works for Kenya and India[11] and Haiti.[12]

Now TOMS has expanded into premium eyewear, which supports vision correction, and more one-for-one models are in the works.[13] In my mind TOMS is not "there" yet, and in fact, such is the case for all of us as we engage the work of doing good, seeking justice, and loving mercy. I have to give some credit to Blake and the executives of TOMS. While I've been one of their early critics, I commend them for the courage to pause, listen to their critics, ask themselves the hard questions, and make important adjustments in their business model. At the end of the day, whether you're for-profit or not-for-profit, we shouldn't do what we do at the expense of those living in poverty.

I may finally wear those TOMS shoes I received as a gift several years ago. Maybe.

C'mon, Gang! Let's Save the World Today!

Scott Bessenecker is a blogger and associate director of missions for InterVarsity Christian Fellowship. His life is about connecting students to issues of justice and compassion, but he has found that motivating them and encouraging them is not a problem.

He says they easily rally around the idea that "we are the generation" to end human trafficking. Or global poverty. Or discrimination. Or fill in the blank.

"I work with college students, helping them to strive after Christ and his kingdom, especially within communities scarred by poverty, hopelessness and exclusion. One of my most daunting challenges is not helping students see that they can make a difference in these complicated situations; it is helping them to confront the messianic complex which convinces them that *they are* the solution."[14]

Bull's-eye.

Bessenecker goes on to point out that in American-made movies, when all of humanity is at risk of extermination through natural disaster or alien attack, it is a wily American who ultimately comes to the rescue.

Do you remember that Tom Cruise/Bruce Willis/Harrison Ford/ Eugene Cho movie in which the planet is under alien attack or faces an epic national disaster and he goes to the UN, makes his case, and recommends that an African or Southeast Asian leader take charge of saving the planet from certain doom?

Yeah, me neither.

Our American triumphalism continues.

Do you think the recipients of our goodwill can see it? Do you think when we enter into conversations with people they can tell that we don't really care about them, exactly, but we just care about "fixing" something that is broken? How would you like it if someone believed you were inherently flawed and needed fixing?

Chimamanda Ngozi Adichie, a Nigerian writer, gave one of the most compelling talks on this subject at a TED event. It is titled

"The Danger of a Single Story." She said, "If I had not grown up in Nigeria, and if all I knew about Africa were from popular images, I too would think that Africa was a place of beautiful landscapes, beautiful animals, and incomprehensible people, fighting senseless wars, dying of poverty and AIDS, unable to speak for themselves and waiting to be saved by a kind, white foreigner."[15]

Preach, Adichie. Preach.

The Responsibility in Storytelling

We've seen the videos, the photos, and the campaigns. For some, the quintessential image of "Africa" is the image of a young boy with a bloated stomach, snot running down his nose, eyes dazed, and flies buzzing around his head. You've seen this image, haven't you?

Never mind that one might have no idea what country these people are from. Ghana, Uganda, or Zimbabwe? They're close to one another, right? There aren't any differences in geography or culture or political context or language, right?

Ugh. I once spoke with a young believer (probably in his twenties or thirties), and he was "all fired up" (his words) about doing something for African orphans in Ghana, and when I asked him where Ghana was, his response was, "Africa."

"Right. Right. But where in Africa?" I asked.

Awkward silence. Blank stare. Very awkward.

We had a good geography lesson that day, but I digress. Now back to the issue of the responsibility in storytelling. Unfortunately, what many of us see or receive is one angle of abject poverty and hopelessness from TV ads, photos, online campaigns, emails, and world news.

Now, I get it. We need resources. In some situations the reality is stark. There's suffering, hardship, and pain. And yes, in some cases, it's a matter of life and death. But let's be honest, many of these images are meant to tug or (manipulate) heartstrings and access wallets, purse strings, and credit cards. While one may push back and contend that the end justifies the means, I would fiercely push back that the cost might be too grave. We can't parade people around the same way the Humane Society parades around abused animals, heap guilt on the audience, and give little dignity to the people we seek to serve.

This happens for causes both near and far, both locally and globally.

So, let's be responsible and work with integrity. It's important because the last thing we want to do is perpetuate the false picture that people in all developing countries are helpless, hopeless, hungry, needy, and incapable.

Are there those who are hungry, thirsty, and living in desperation? Unfortunately … yes. But such can be said of those in our respective countries in the West too, even sadly and poignantly in the country that I call home.

Time and time again, an African friend or colleague has challenged me—passionately, politely, and at times angrily—on something that is captured perfectly by this email sent by a good friend from South Africa:

Eugene,

We know you run a development and humanitarian organization. Thank you for your work, but as you share the stories of difficulties and pain, don't forget to share the stories of beauty, hope, courage, and love.

Please be responsible in your storytelling.

Please tell your Western countries that Africa is not a dangerous place, full of warmongers and child soldiers, and starving, helpless, and desperate people. Please tell your folks that while we appreciate love, prayers, and support, we are not in need of the "Western White Saviors."

We are proud. We are beautiful. We have a history; we have beautiful stories and songs. We are not perfect but we, too, are created in the wondrous image of God.

This is a truth I have to keep reminding myself again and again. And I hope this speaks to you as well.

Chimamanda communicated in her TED presentation:

> The single story creates stereotypes, and the problem with stereotypes is not that they are untrue, but that they are incomplete. They make one story become the only story....
>
> Stories matter. Many stories matter. Stories have been used to dispossess and to malign, but stories can also be used to empower and to humanize. Stories can break the dignity of a people, but stories can also repair that broken dignity.[16]

Imagine if other countries sent their missionaries, NGOs, and churches to your respective country. What if they came to the United States? Perhaps in response to the ridiculous government shutdown that took place in October 2013.

Imagine African or Asian NGOs and churches arriving in the States to save us because we were shut down. They would likely take lots of selfies with us smiling or crying in the background. They would take photos of us with runny noses, ripped Abercrombies, and worn-out TOMS shoes. Maybe they would sell T-shirts to save us. #AfricanSaviorComplex

Sounds ridiculous, right?

Stories matter. How we communicate those stories matters. Our choices in the photos we capture and parade on our websites, brochures, and campaigns matter. Our choice to use photos of real children, women, or men on T-shirts, and to sell them for good causes matters. Asking ourselves the questions, "Should we do it?" and "What were we thinking?" matters, even if we have their permission. We need to question this practice and consider the stories we're telling. I mean, seriously, would you want photos of your children being paraded around on clothing worn by strangers?

My point is that to reduce the tapestry, identity, narrative, history, and fabric of an entire country or continent (comprised of many different countries) to one image or marketing angle is irresponsible, dangerous, and wrong. Even if that angle might be accurate in itself, to convey that angle without the context of a larger story is dangerous.

Whether our cause is a country in Africa, a country in Asia, the Middle East, Latin America, South America, or in our own cities and neighborhoods involving teen pregnancy, and homelessness, education disparity, we have to ask the question: How are we telling the stories of the people we serve?

And once you ask that question, you have to ask it again and again and again.

The Singular Story of the Suspicious, Scary Black Man?

Some years ago, I recall having a very raw and honest conversation with one of my congregants at Quest Church. To be more specific, I was having a conversation with a young African American congregant—one of the few at Quest, if I'm honest.

He shared this story that remains seared in my mind:

> Pastor Eugene, you often speak of injustice, racism, and prejudice. Thank you for sharing your story. I wanted to also share my story with you. In fact, I feel my "otherness" every single day. Every single day.
>
> You see, I get on the Metro Bus early on its transit up north as it makes its way south to downtown Seattle where I work. As you can imagine, the bus eventually gets crowded. In fact, it gets packed. But when I get on the bus, I am always among the first ten passengers, and each of us can choose where to sit. And yes, we all choose to sit ... alone. But as the bus makes it way from stop to stop, I begin to notice something. People are eager to find seats, and every single day, every seat is taken ... but nearly every single day ... one seat remains ...

the last seat taken. Can you guess which seat that is? Yes, it is the seat next to me. It is the last seat taken. Nearly every single day. Do you know why? Do you know why? … It's because I am a dark-skinned black man … and people believe I am dangerous. This is how I begin my day. Nearly every day. This is my story.

This is an example of the hidden injustice and danger of the singular story.

Many of us—and likely all of us—have had certain perceptions imposed upon us without even knowing that our lens of seeing race and others has been distorted.

If we're completely honest, all too often, black men—especially young black men—are seen through the singular story that they are suspicious and scary, if not dangerous. And this, in itself, is unjust. This is racist.

Acting Only on Instinct: The Road to Hell

You and I probably can't imagine the terror of being in Port-au-Prince, Haiti, on January 12, 2010. As people were just beginning their day, a massive 7.0 magnitude earthquake rocked the capital city and the surrounding area. The shoddily built city crumbled, killing two hundred thousand people as numerous concrete buildings collapsed.[17]

This catastrophic disaster affected about three million Haitians.[18] The temblor crippled the country, already fragile in its infrastructure and economy.

For several days after the earthquake, news coverage documented rescue efforts around the clock, and stories of loss and redemption from the rubble were reported.[19] Neighborhood heroes dug out orphaned children. Husbands rescued their wives from the wreckage.[20]

The stories and images prompted a massive wave of support, both financial and otherwise. And for at least a few people, the goodwill took a very physical form.

Working on instinct, one Puerto Rican businessman packed a barge filled with food and other supplies and sent it to Port-au-Prince after hearing about the devastation. Once the barge arrived, aid workers in Haiti found it was poorly packed and contained items such as potato chips and grape juice. Not the kind of stuff that would be helpful after a disaster. The barge was a mess, taking the time of many humanitarian workers to sort and unpack the items, many of which were not critical in responding to a disaster of this magnitude.

For several weeks the barge took up precious dock space in Port-au-Prince, space that could have been used to off-load vessels with desperately needed emergency supplies.

The well-meaning businessman acted only on instinct, very likely not consulting with experts in the field as to what supplies would be valuable in an emergency. No attempt at coordinating the delivery was made—until the barge was already sailing toward the disaster.

In frustration, considering the barge, one aid worker said that while the man who sent it had good intentions, "The road to hell is paved with good intentions."[21]

Stronger Together

That's not to say there were no successes amid the disaster. I believe a sign of successful justice work is the realization that we are stronger when we work together, when we believe there is strength in partnership.

One example of this kind of effort is the hospital being built by Partners In Health (PIH), an organization that strives to be just that: A partner with Haiti's government. Located in the town of Mirebalais, some thirty miles from the capital, Partners In Health rebuilt a hospital. This orchestration of Haiti's biggest reconstruction project in the health sector was designed specifically with the people's needs in mind.

An article in *The Nation* quoted David Walton, who was then a thirty-two-year-old doctor from Brigham and Women's Hospital in Boston: "The officials we are dealing with are clever, cooperative and motivated," said Walton, as he surveyed the progress. "And they have ideas. But nobody listens to them. Few NGOs even try working with the government. It is much simpler to work around them."[22]

I visited Port-au-Prince in the months following, to see for myself how One Day's Wages was helping people rebuild. I was encouraged by the work of our partner agencies, rebuilding homes and supporting Haitians as they recovered.

Haiti is one of the countries in great need of thoughtful assistance, done in partnership and driven by locals who are invested in the success of the work. I was struck, as many people are, by the need for investment in real solutions.

Relief, Recovery, or Development?

Anyone who is seriously interested in learning a biblical perspective of helping the poor responsibly should read *When Helping Hurts*. It challenges a lot of assumptions about development, getting to the fact that true transformation must be lived and breathed. They describe good development as setting people in the right relationship with God, self, others, and the rest of creation.

One of the other big takeaways of the book for me is to always be circumspect about how and why we embark on any sort of assistance to the poor. In the book the authors provide clarity in the differences between relief, recovery, and development.

A helpful first step in thinking about working with the poor in any context is to discern whether the situation calls for relief, rehabilitation, or development. The failure to distinguish among these situations is one of the most common reasons that poverty-alleviation efforts often do harm.

Relief is the urgent and temporary provision of emergency aid to reduce immediate suffering from a natural or man-made crisis; to stop the bleeding—the Good Samaritan.

Rehabilitation is seeking to restore people and their communities to the positive elements of their precrisis conditions; and the key element is to work with the victims as they participate in their own recovery.

Development is the process of ongoing change that moves all the people involved—both the "helpers" and the "helped"—closer to being in right relationship with God, self, others, and the rest of creation; this is not done to or for people but with people.[23]

Let's look at an example. In 2004, all hell was breaking loose in western Sudan, in a region known as Darfur. As anyone who follows current events will know, men on horseback, the Janjaweed, were committing mind-boggling atrocities against entire villages.

They were fueled by a hatred made up of spiritual, racial, and political differences between themselves and the villagers. Sudan's own president, Omar al-Bashir, was shown to be funding the Janjaweed and has since been indicted for crimes against humanity.[24]

The "devils on horseback" often raped any women they found, killed indiscriminately, and used torches to light the thatch-roofed huts on fire. It was as if Satan visited these villages, robbing people of their dignity and livelihoods, and their very lives. As a result, when the Janjaweed came close to a village, people in the community would flee for their lives into the bush, hiding and trying to save themselves from the terror that was soon to envelop their village.

In the weeks and months following these attacks, humanitarian groups entered western Sudan and eastern Chad, seeking the traumatized survivors. As with any large-scale humanitarian initiative, some things went well and some did not, but this context provides us with a background to see some key differences in response.

At the outset, humanitarian groups offered emergency assistance to the refugees and displaced people, including food and temporary shelter. These broken families were not able to bring much with them; perhaps a few cooking pots, a sleeping pad, and an animal or two—if they were fortunate.

This initial phase is called *relief*, when we are able to help people through a crisis that they cannot handle on their own. The Red Cross provides relief in the United States, providing assistance immediately following a house fire, for example, offering families who have lost everything a moment to regroup.

However, this initial phase of emergency assistance is often where we stop. We do not move beyond handouts. This is our Western mind-set about helping people: to be content with giving handouts instead of equipping people long-term. In reality, this initial phase of relief should be time limited, likely only one to three months.

Beyond relief, we need *recovery*—life rehabilitation—to bring people to at least the level they were before the crisis. What was missing from the lives of Darfur refugees? Much. One of the most critical elements was the means and access to grow their own food. A key point in the rehabilitation phase is that it is not a one-way street. The job of the humanitarians is not providing food; it is training and equipping those in need to do it on their own.

Once individuals are able to reach a survival level similar to where they were predisaster, a truly compassionate aid worker will work through the complexities of life with them, to ensure they are better off than before. This phase is called *development*. This is my favorite phase.

In the context of the Darfur refugees, development came in the form of skill training, savings groups, and microlending to grow businesses.

One simple and powerful way to begin saving in this cultural context is through a revolving loan—or tontine, as it is called in the region. The basic concept is this: Four women get together, and every week, they throw in a dollar. Every week, one of the women receives four dollars, which she can then invest in something such as a pot for cooking or a tool for farming.

God-given ingenuity takes over in this development phase. A friend of mine at World Concern met a man named Saboune in a refugee camp in eastern Chad. Saboune lost everything in the retreat from the Janjaweed—everything, that is, except for his tenacity.

Thanks to some initial investments from World Concern and Saboune's background in business, he leveraged a small loan for a pushcart into a cart-rental business. He saved his income from the carts and eventually opened a general store.

In the middle of a refugee camp, Saboune was selling pasta, buckets, beans, spices, and more. With his income, Saboune was able to care for his family and extended family—thirteen children. He was able to retain things that are impossible to buy—his smile and his pride—knowing that even though his life had been turned upside down, he was regaining control over his future.

These are responsible ways to respond to a hurting world, but true change is even deeper. Brian Fikkert has indicated in an article in *Christianity Today* that the need for more capital and better technology persists.[25] But we must realize that God created us for more.

True transformation is to be reconciled to God, our community, and others.

> People really do need improved access to clean water, better health care, decent education, and a living wage. But they, and we, need something far more profound. Whether we realize it or not, we all are longing for an intimate relationship with God, for a sense of dignity, for community and

belonging, and for the ability to use our gifts and abilities to develop creation.[26]

Relationships > Missions

The movement toward missions in US churches astounds me. It's a wonderful, yet complicated area of growth.

About twenty-five years ago, one hundred twenty thousand people embarked on short-term mission trips, usually spending one to three weeks in an impoverished area or country, serving the community in some way. Now the number of short-term missionaries has grown by at least 1,800 percent to about 2.2 million in 2006. That year, we spent 1.6 billion on the trips alone.[27]

Given this astounding growth, I have two general reactions:

First, wow, it's great how the Spirit is moving. Second, let's consider the impact. With any massive change in behavior, there must be impact, with both good and bad consequences, intentional and unintentional.

As some of you are aware, the ministry of "short-term missions" is part of the ethos of many churches and religious organizations. Many churches sponsor these short-term teams who travel to places—often to economically challenged communities, both locally and globally—for one or two weeks, hoping to engage in service projects and various forms of evangelism. These trips are often designed mostly for teens and college students, and sometimes include adults. But let's ask the question: *Why* do we send teams on short-team missions?

A couple of stories stand out in my mind when I think of mission trips gone wrong. There is the church in Mexico that was hosting many short-term mission teams and allowed its building to be repainted six times during one summer by six different groups. The short-term teams stayed busy that summer.

Then there was a misguided short-term missions team in Brazil who accidentally built a wall on an orphanage's soccer field.[28]

I know good work is being done on short-term missions. However, could the locals do the work that is done by short-term teams?

The typical short-term mission trip might easily cost between $2,000 and $4,000 per person. The thought of sending ten to twenty people from a church across the world at a cost of between $20,000 and $80,000 doesn't make a lot of sense when you consider how far that money would go if given directly to fund in-country development initiatives. In many places a salary for a local humanitarian or church worker might be $1,500—that's the *annual* salary and also the cost of one international airline ticket.

Still, I know the value in seeing the world, as my experiences in the developing world forced me to reevaluate my own life. After I met people and learned their stories, I could not help but be changed.

It is critical to evaluate whether your work is sustainable, and to consider how much you spend on various aspects of the work. Spending *more* money to visit in person and *see* the work than you are *investing* in the work is ludicrous.

Some in the missions community have pushed back on international short-term missions because they are so expensive. The money spent can go further closer to home, they say.

I personally don't believe we need to choose between international and domestic. I believe *neighbor* is a broad term, especially now because we know about and are connected with the entire planet through the web, nonstop cable news, and social media.

While it still may be a bad idea to send a team of twenty to Mexico to repaint a church wall, the value in international travel and "vision trips" remains.

Don't Reduce People to Projects

As I ask these questions, I don't want to miss something important.

It is easy for us, perhaps more so with our individualistic Western mind-set, to forget that relationships matter. Acknowledging and hearing someone's story matters.

We have to be particularly careful—locally, globally, or perhaps within our own communities—how we engage those we serve.

We have to constantly remember that they, too, are created in the image of God. Someone I am less likely to consider helpless and in need of saving. Someone to come alongside of. Someone full of potential. Someone God created. Someone with a story. Someone who might be able to teach me.

This is the importance of dignity, mutuality, and reciprocity, or in more simple terms, we acknowledge their human worth and beauty. We have things to both learn from and teach one another, and we are in relationship with one another.

Be careful. Be wise. Be human.

When you start dehumanizing the poor, you have no desire to build relationships with them. You have no interest in their stories. You have no interest in relationships. You believe stereotypes that others have told you about them. You believe the lie that they have nothing to teach us and are incapable of contributing to the larger society.

When you're not interested in building genuine mutual relationships, you rob people of their dignity and they become projects. Don't reduce people into projects. When that happens, they become statistics instead of people. How can you love and serve the poor if you don't even know the poor?

As Shane Claiborne wrote in his book *The Irresistible Revolution*, "I think that's what our world is desperately in need of—lovers, people who are building deep, genuine relationships with fellow strugglers along the way, and who actually know the faces of the people behind the issues they are concerned about."[29]

On the morning of one of our church's recent Thanksgiving meals, I heard some unfortunate news. Initially, I read it through the local neighborhood blogs and then the local papers:

> A man's body was found Saturday morning in Ballard, but police said there were no signs of foul play.[30]

The dead man was found in Ballard Commons Park across from the Ballard branch library and two blocks from NW Market Street. This is less than a mile from the Bridge Care Center—our church's homeless advocacy and justice center. His identity wasn't immediately known, but police said he was "a transient who frequented the park."

It's sad when a person passes away and hardly anyone notices, and even more so when his or her death is announced without a name and that person is simply described as a "transient." It's not a criticism of the paper, because they had absolutely no knowledge of or relationship with this person. As more information became known, it turns out that this unnamed and "transient" person was a friend of the Bridge. Although I did not know him very well, I explained to our church that a fellow brother in our community had passed away.

His name was Don.

Jill, one of our staff members and the director of our advocacy center, knew him well and grieved over his passing. Rather than the brief and impersonal sentences in the local paper, I wanted to share her words and description of Don as a way to honor him and the thousands of homeless people who die on the streets of our communities:

Dear Volunteers,

We were blessed to have seventy-five of our homeless brothers and sisters join us in the Quest basement for a beautiful feast last night. It was great to feel the community and love that was buzzing around the room. I was so thankful to have so many wonderful Quest volunteers who were eager to love and serve.

While yesterday was an opportunity to "rejoice with those who rejoice," it was also a time to "mourn with those who mourn." I wanted to let you know that I found out yesterday that one of our regular clients of the Bridge passed away yesterday morning. Our friend Don was found at Ballard skate park early yesterday morning. It is not a definite as to what the cause of his death was. Byron had been with him during the night, and they had been drinking. He was also exposed to the rain that night, and it got pretty cold. I had also heard Don had some heart issues, so it really could have been a combination of it all. Whatever the cause, this came as a complete shock to me.

For those of you who remember Don, he was always well put together. He was one of our regular Native American clients. His hair often reminded me of the eighties, with his gray ponytail and buzzed cut up on top. I hardly ever remember him without his glasses and a baseball cap on. He often had a job. He was kind and engaging to his friends and all of the volunteers at the Bridge. Don truly will be missed!

While it is never easy to deal with death, I consider it an honor to grieve with the rest of our homeless friends who lost a great friend yesterday. I read of Don's passing in the Seattle PI, *and while I don't blame them for not knowing him, it's very hard to read "police said he was a transient who frequented the park." I am so glad that Don was more than just a transient to us. He was our friend.*

Please keep Don's friends and family (I believe he had five kids) in prayer …

People matter. Never forget.

Chapter 10

THE BEST PART OF WANTING TO CHANGE THE WORLD

Tales of a broken world are all around, and it's easy to be discouraged, but take heart. The gospel is such that God loves the world. Christ came. Christ died. Christ rose … and Christ will return again. What does this mean?

God is still speaking to the world.

God is still speaking to the church.

God is still speaking to His daughters and sons.

I believe this with every fiber of my being. God is still speaking, stirring, and calling His people to be a part of what He is doing … here, there, and everywhere.

The questions for us to ponder are twofold:

Are we still listening to Him?

(Thus, the exhortation for us to "shut up, listen, and pray.")

And, do we have the courage to pray and live this prayer? "Thank You, Lord, for the convictions You speak into our hearts. Now, give us the courage to act upon those convictions."

We Can't Just Love the Idea

Ideas, in and of themselves, don't change the world.

Rather, people who faithfully and tenaciously implement their ideas change the world. Women, men, and children who have the courage to pursue their convictions change the world. That's you and me. It's those who respond. For those who are Christians, worship isn't just ingestion of good news—worship and discipleship begins when we respond to the revelation of God. When we choose to live out our faith.

That idea in your head?

Pray about it.

Reflect on it.

Get it out.

Talk about it.

Test it.

Share it.

Put flesh to it.

Pursue it.

Implement it.

Ultimately, if we believe God has called us to something, we must go for it.

I once read a quote from Jon Klinepeter, a pastor in Chicago, which he had posted online, and I scribbled it on a notepad. I'll let it speak for itself:

> If only Facebook had always been around, our broken world would have been fixed long ago. All you have to do to make the world a better place is to change your profile picture or status update. Just think, Dr. King wouldn't have needed to march. Gandhi wouldn't have gone on a hunger strike. And Mother Teresa would have never needed to actually touch a sick or poor person. They could have just let everyone know their opinion on FB and everything would have changed for the better.

We can't just be in love with the idea of changing the world.

When we are faithful to what God wants us to do, beautiful things happen. No, I am not suggesting that everything we will do must appear successful by the world's standards of success. Our work may not be huge. It may not grow to a massive size and scale. It may not garner the attention and affection of media. It doesn't have to be about those things. It will likely not be easy … but it will be beautiful nevertheless because we will have been faithful to the Lord's call.

I'm stirred by the words of the apostle Paul in Philippians 4:8: "Finally, brothers and sisters, whatever is true, whatever is noble, whatever is right, whatever is pure, whatever is lovely, whatever is admirable—if anything is excellent or praiseworthy—think about such things."

Think about such things.

Engage in these things.

Our natural tendency as humans is to quit or alter our course the minute we see opposition, barriers, or setbacks. When we do this, we don't put flesh to our dreams. Our dreams remain just an idea. They don't come to life on their own.

Let's be honest: No single one of us can change the entire world, but we can impact the worlds of some. In fact, I contend that we need to do away with the "I can change the whole world" mentality and language because it's impossible, and actually unhelpful. But we can impact the worlds of some. And some may be many. Some may be just a few. Some may be just one family or one person, but we can make an impact and in the process, *be changed ourselves*. This, in my opinion, is the best part of wanting to change the world. Inevitably, we will be changed in the process.

We need to have a theology of discipleship and a theology of justice that inform our praxis of discipleship.

We need to be soaked in the grace of God that informs and transforms who we are and how we seek to live our lives. Grace changes everything. Most important and most miraculously, it changes us.

We need to shut up, listen, and pray.

We need to commit to going deep, learning, growing, and being experts in the areas to which God has called us.

We need to act.

Gary Haugen, in his book *Just Courage*, framed the invitation as simply as possible:

> He is inviting all of us on His great, costly expedition of transformation in the world—but we must

respond. Are we coming or staying? Jesus is relent-
lessly issuing the invitation and forcing a choice to
action. What are we doing to *do*? I am much more
interested in telling Jesus and others what I *believe*,
but Jesus (and the watching world) know that what
I truly believe will be manifested in what I choose
to *do*.[1]

Sometimes the most significant things we can do to change the
world involve how we live our lives every day.

Sometimes we're so obsessed with wanting to do earth-shattering
things that we can forget the mundane and simple things. As we
engage the larger world, let's not forget to befriend, love, and serve
those in our own backyards.

If we truly want to change the world, we can begin with …

Our families.

Our neighbors.

Our communities.

Some people will scoff at the idea of changing the world, and in
many ways, I would agree with the cynics. I am a recovering cynic
myself. But believe this: We must act. We must start somewhere. A
movement always begins with a single step.

Mother Teresa, who impacted the lives of so many, realized this:
"Never worry about numbers. Help one person at a time and always
start with the person nearest you."[2]

In fact, Mother Teresa also shared this simple and profound
encouragement: "What can you do to promote world peace? Go
home and love your family."[3]

In Western culture and even in our churches, we can get so obsessed with success, growth, organizations, scaling, and metrics that we neglect the simple, small, and ordinary things. We have to be faithful in the small things. We're so obsessed with oceans and mighty floods that we forget that little ripples of faith, hope, and love can change the world.

"Jesus welcomes our ordinary offerings because it's the ordinary things that best teach about faith and sacrifice," wrote Leroy Barber in his book *Everyday Missions*. "It's also the ordinary things that point out the holes in our society—the things that should not be accepted as normal. Ordinary offerings do not go unnoticed by God; in fact, God can use ordinary offerings to change the world."[4]

It's true. When you look throughout the Scriptures, the stories are often about the nobodies, the have-nots, and the misfits. Consider the background of those whom we elevate as spiritual heroes. They were, in fact, all ordinary people who simply offered their ordinary lives—some with great reticence and trepidation.

Adam and Eve lied, concealed, and accused. Abraham was old and had some serious marriage issues. Noah was a drunk. Jacob was insecure. Joseph was abused and sold into slavery. Moses had a stuttering and confidence problem—and was also a murderer. Elijah was depressed. Gideon was poor. Rahab was a prostitute. David had a list too long for this book. Jonah was rebellious and unwilling to listen to God's instructions. John the Baptist was John the Baptist. Martha was a workaholic. The Samaritan woman had numerous failed relationships and was ostracized in her community. Thomas had doubts. Matthew was a tax collector. Paul was a Pharisee. And Timothy was timid.

If there's one thing you take away from this book, I hope it is this: Don't underestimate what God can do through your life. God has a long and proven history of using foolish and broken people for His glory.

Fascinate, Not Force, People Toward the Gospel

Our lives matter. How we live our lives, our depth, our prayer, our integrity, our willingness to do what we ask others to do, it all matters. I would like for people to see me and, through that, see the glory of God. One day I want Jesus to say, "Well done, My faithful servant."

Notice that in Matthew 25:21, Jesus didn't say, "Well done, My successful servant." Let's be faithful.

I know that when people see me, they will see an imperfect and broken person. One of my goals in life is to fascinate people and direct them toward the gospel by my actions, by my perseverance and commitment to do what is right. I want people to think, *What is going on here?* And for us as believers, that something is a *Someone* and that Someone is *Jesus*.

Rather than fear, guilt, or shame, let's inspire people with hope, beauty, and courage. Let's fascinate, not force, people toward the gospel.

Don't just tell us what you're against.

Demonstrate what you're about.

Fascinate us.

Compel us.

Invite us.

Help us reimagine a better story.

When we started Quest Church in 2001, Minhee and I could not have envisioned the journey ahead. The people we have met since and the relationships we've formed in community—it's all too emotional to recount. Through it all, we've seen God move in both thunderous and quiet ways. As I write this chapter, I think of a recent event: We had a young mother at Quest who shared her testimony before her baptism this past Sunday. She shared about the "gaping hole" she had felt in her heart her whole life and how she had sought to satisfy this hole with things, relationships, chemicals, or food. It was in coming to Quest that she somehow encountered Jesus, and all along, it was He whom she'd longed for.

Oh, the journey.

When Minhee and I were convicted to start One Day's Wages, my personal thought was singular and specific: *God wants* me *to change the world.*

I need to help these people. I need to solve the issue of extreme poverty. I need to create this organization. It's embarrassing to confess, but as I look back, much of this thinking revolved around me.

I honestly felt that God wanted me to change the world. Now while I still believe that there's an element of truth in this—because let's face it, there is work to be done—in hindsight, I've learned that God called us into this journey not just to "change the world" but more so to change us.

And wow … has God changed us!

And God is continuing to change us.

I am learning again and again that this is what discipleship is all about. I believe this because I've seen it in my life: The best part about wanting to change the world is that you will get changed in the process.

Last Thoughts

Thanks for reading this book. Sincerely, thank you.

Take a moment, or two, or some time to pause, listen, and pray. Ask yourself the hard questions. Do the due diligence and research required for you to be an expert or a person of depth in the areas of your passion and conviction. Then pray some more. Take the time to listen and ask many questions. Be teachable. Learn. Consider those who have gone before you. Don't reinvent the wheel. Seek counsel. *Then go for it.*

Repeat. Keep learning. Keep praying. Have courage. Be tenacious. Go for it, but don't stop taking the time to shut up, listen, pray, and act.

That's my cue to do the same.

NOTES

Chapter 1—Couch Surfing: Our Story

1. Ben Schiller, "Like a Charity on Facebook? You're Now Less Likely to Actually Help," *Fast Company*, November 13, 2003, www.fastcoexist.com/3021508/heres-an-idea/like-a-charity-on-facebook-youre-now-actually-less-to-actually-help.

Chapter 2—Why We Do Justice

1. Timothy Keller, *Generous Justice: How God's Grace Makes Us Just* (New York: Penguin, 2010), 3.

2. Ken Wytsma, *Pursuing Justice: The Call to Live and Die for Bigger Things* (Nashville: Thomas Nelson, 2013), 9.

3. Wytsma, *Pursuing Justice*, 9.

4. Gary A. Haugen, *Just Courage: God's Great Expedition for the Restless Christian* (Downers Grove, IL: InterVarsity Press, 2009), 75.

5. Keller, *Generous Justice*, 3–4.

6. Keller, *Generous Justice*, 142.

7. Jean Highland, ed., *The Words of Martin Luther King, Jr.*, 2nd ed. (New York: Newmarket, 2008), 66.

8. Keller, *Generous Justice*, 67–68.

Chapter 3—The Tension of Upward Mobility: We Are Blessed

1. "Mammon," *Wikipedia*, http://en.wikipedia.org/wiki/Mammon.

2. "National Average Wage Index," Social Security, www.ssa.gov/OACT/COLA/AWI.html.

3. "Poverty Overview," The World Bank, April 7, 2014, http://web.worldbank.org/WBSITE/EXTERNAL/TOPICS/EXTPOVERTY/EXTPA/0,,contentMDK:200

40961~menuPK:435040~pagePK:148956~piPK:216618~theSitePK:430367~isC URL:Y,00.html.

4. "Poverty Overview."

5. "Progress on Sanitation and Drinking-Water: 2013 Update," World Health Organization/UNICEF, www.wssinfo.org/fileadmin/user_upload/resources/JMPreport 2013.pdf.

6. "Progress on Sanitation."

7. "Goal 5: Improve Maternal Health," United Nations: We Can End Poverty, www.un.org/millenniumgoals/maternal.shtml.

8. U2, "Stand Up Comedy," *No Line on the Horizon*, © 2009 Mercury.

9. "Poverty Statistics," Gospel Justice Initiative, www.gji.org/learn/poverty-statistics.

10. Norman Herr, "Television & Health," The Sourcebook for Teaching Science, www.csun.edu/science/health/docs/tv&health.html.

11. "G. K. Chesterton Quotes," Goodreads, www.goodreads.com/quotes/73243-there -are-two-ways-to-get-enough-one-is-to.

12. Ronald J. Sider, *Rich Christians in an Age of Hunger: Moving from Affluence to Generosity* (Nashville: Thomas Nelson, 1977), 186.

13. Richard J. Foster, *The Challenge of the Disciplined Life: Christian Reflections on Money, Sex, & Power* (New York: HarperCollins, 1989), 44.

14. Foster, *Challenge of the Disciplined Life*, 35.

15. John C. Maxwell, *The 21 Indispensable Qualities of a Leader: Becoming the Person Others Will Want to Follow* (Nashville: Thomas Nelson), 63.

16. Richard J. Foster, *Freedom of Simplicity: Finding Harmony in a Complex World* (New York: HarperCollins, 2010), 58.

17. Blake Ellis, "Class of 2013 Grads Average $35,200 in Total Debt," May 17, 2003, CNN Money, http://money.cnn.com/2013/05/17/pf/college/student-debt /index.html.

18. Ylan Q. Mui, "Credit Card Reform Has Companies Treading Lightly on Campus," *Washington Post*, August 27, 2010, www.washingtonpost.com/wp-dyn/content /article/2010/08/26/AR2010082604058.html.

19. Fred O. Williams, "Average Credit Card Debt? Take Your Pick," CreditCards.com, July 8, 2013, www.creditcards.com/credit-card-news/average-credit_card_debt -1276.php.

20. Williams, "Average Credit Card Debt?"

21. "Guestbook Messages," Yahn & Son Funeral Home and Crematory: Obituaries, http://yahnandson.myfuneralwebsite.com/pages/show_printable_content.php?site id=122&action=1&value=12&menuitem=1283&obituaries_action=17&obituaryi d=118076&obituaries_page=15.

Chapter 4—Shut Up, Listen, and Pray

1. "Who Watches What (and How Much?): U.S. TV Trends by Ethnicity," Nielson, March 30, 2011, www.nielsen.com/us/en/newswire/2011/who-watches-what-and -how-much-u-s-tv-trends-by-ethnicity.html.

2. Norman Herr, "Television & Health," The Sourcebook for Teaching Science, www.csun.edu/science/health/docs/tv&health.html.

3. Becky Benenate and Jospeh Durepos, eds., *Mother Teresa: No Greater Love* (Novato, CA: New World Library, 2002), 8.

4. Richard J. Foster, *Streams of Living Water: Celebrating the Great Traditions of Christian Faith* (San Francisco: HarperCollins, 1988), 173.

5. Gary A. Haugen, *Just Courage: God's Great Expedition for the Restless Christian* (Downers Grove, IL: InterVarsity Press, 2009), 23.

6. Henri J. M. Nouwen, *Life of the Beloved: Spiritual Living in a Secular World* (New York: Crossroads, 2002), 110.

7. "C. S. Lewis Quotes," Goodreads, www.goodreads.com/quotes/28672-i-know -now-lord-why-you-utter-no-answer-you.

Chapter 6—Asking the Hard Questions: Self-Examination

1. Timothy Keller, *Generous Justice: How God's Grace Makes Us Just* (New York: Penguin, 2010), 112.

2. Jean Highland, ed., *The Words of Martin Luther King, Jr.*, 2nd ed. (New York: Newmarket, 2008), 51.

3. Jon Krakauer, "Three Cups of Deceit," Byliner, www.byliner.com/originals/three-cups-of-deceit.

4. Jon Krakauer, "Is It Time to Forgive Greg Mortenson?" The Daily Beast, April 8, 2013, www.thedailybeast.com/articles/2013/04/08/is-it-time-to-forgive-greg-mortenson.html.

5. Michael Daly, "The Death of Co-Author of 'Three Cups of Tea' Is Ruled Suicide," The Daily Beast, December 6, 2012, www.thedailybeast.com/articles/2012/12/06/the-death-of-co-author-of-three-cups-of-tea-is-ruled-suicide.html.

6. Nicholas D. Kristof, "'Three Cups of Tea,' Spilled," The Opinion Pages, *New York Times*, April 20, 2011, www.nytimes.com/2011/04/21/opinion/21kristof.html.

7. Shane Claiborne, *The Irresistible Revolution: Living as an Ordinary Radical* (Grand Rapids, MI: Zondervan, 2006), 132.

Chapter 7—Having More Depth Than 140 Characters: Be an Expert

1. "Óscar Romero," *Wikipedia*, http://en.wikipedia.org/wiki/%C3%93scar_Romero.

2. "Religions: Liberation Theology," BBC, July 18, 2011, www.bbc.co.uk/religion/religions/christianity/beliefs/liberationtheology.shtml.

3. "Murder of Vincent Chin," *Wikipedia*, http://en.wikipedia.org/wiki/Murder_of_Vincent_Chin.

4. "2013 Street Count Results," Seattle/King County Coalitions on Homelessness, www.homelessinfo.org/what_we_do/one_night_count/2013_results.php.

5. See "About Homelessness," Operation Nightwatch, www.seattlenightwatch.org/homelessness.htm.

6. Shane Claiborne, *The Irresistible Revolution: Living as an Ordinary Radical* (Grand Rapids, MI: Zondervan, 2006), 295.

7. Luis Andres Henao, "Jan Eliasson, UN Deputy Chief, Urges Action on Global Water Crisis," *Huffington Post*, January 28, 2013, www.huffingtonpost.com/2013/01/25/jan-eliasson-un-water-rights_n_2551266.html?utm_hp_ref=clean-water.

8. "Cholera," World Health Organization, February 2014, www.who.int/mediacentre /factsheets/fs107/en/.

9. Brian Merchant, "Up to 60% of Water Wells in Developing World Don't Work (Video)," Treehugger, October 25, 2010, www.treehugger.com/corporate-responsibility /up-to-60-of-water-wells-in-developing-world-dont-work-video.html.

10. "Providing Clean Water," World Concern, http://worldconcern.org/myconcern /water.

11. Henao, "Jan Eliasson."

12. Rachel Bonham Carter, "WASH Initiative Highlights African Women's Needs for Improved Water and Sanitation," UNICEF, September 15, 2005, www.unicef .org/wash/index_28268.html.

Chapter 8—Don't Ask Others to Do What You're Not Willing to Do Yourself

1. Reuters, "Pope Chooses Simple Residence over Regal Papal Apartment," NBC News, March 26, 2013, http://worldnews.nbcnews.com/_news/2013/03/26/17477922-pope -chooses-simple -residence-over-regal-papal-apartment?lite.

2. Amanda Enayati, "For Kids, It's Better to Give than Receive," CNN Living, September 17, 2012, www.cnn.com/2012/09/17/living/giving-makes-children-happy.

3. "Altruism & Happiness," PBS, *This Emotional Life*, www.pbs.org/thisemotionallife /topic/altruism/altruism-happiness. See also Tara Parker-Pope, "The Generous Marriage," *New York Times*, December 8, 2011, http://well.blogs.nytimes.com/2011 /12/08/is-generosity-better-than-sex/.

4. Mfonobong Nsehe, "Nigeria's Richest Pastor Puts Private Jets Up for Sale," *Forbes*, August 4, 2011, www.forbes.com/sites/mfonobongnsehe/2011/08/04/nigerias-richest -pastor-puts-private-jets-up-for-sale/.

5. Mfonobong Nsehe, "Wealthy Nigerians, Pastors Spend $225 Million on Private Jets," *Forbes*, May 17, 2011, www.forbes.com/sites/mfonobongnsehe/2011/05/17 /wealthy-nigerians-pastors-spend-225-million-on-private-jets/.

6. Anji, "Shave Anji's Head!" One Day's Wages, http://www.onedayswages.org/donate /org/shave-anjis-head.

7. Anji, "Shave Anji's Head!"

8. "Joon's Campaign for a Cause," One Day's Wages, www.onedayswages.org/donate
/org/joons-campaign-cause.

9. From Wylie's website, Pedal Across America for Clean Water, http://pedalacros-
samerica.wordpress.com/about/.

Chapter 9—The Irony of Doing Justice ...
Unjustly

1. Ken Wytsma with D. R. Jacobsen, *Pursuing Justice: The Call to Live and Die for
Bigger Things* (Nashville: Thomas Nelson, 2013), 157.

2. Steve Corbett and Brian Fikkert, *When Helping Hurts: How to Alleviate Poverty
Without Hurting the Poor ... and Yourself* (Chicago: Moody, 2009), 65.

3. Corbett and Fikkert, *When Helping Hurts*, 65.

4. "Comin' Thro' the Rye," *Wikipedia*, http://en.wikipedia.org/wiki/Comin%27
_Thro%27_the_Rye.

5. "TV Commercial – Skechers – Bobs – Featuring Brooke Burke Charvet,"
YouTube video, 0.15, www.youtube.com/watch?v=1x2XsABiMxw.

6. Jeff Chu, "TOMS Sets Out to Sell a Lifestyle, Not Just Shoes," *Fast Company*,
June 17, 2013, www.fastcompany.com/3012568/blake-mycoskie-toms.

7. Isaac Otto, "TOMS Shoes Responds to Critics, But It May Not Be
Enough," Global Envision, July 24, 2013, www.globalenvision.org/2013/07/23
/toms-shoes-responds-critics-it-may-not-be-enough.

8. Adriana Herrera, "Questioning the TOMS Shoes Model for Social Enterprise,"
You're the Boss, *New York Times*, March 19, 2013, http://boss.blogs.nytimes.
com/2013/03/19/questioning-the-toms-shoes-model-for-social-enterprise/?_php
=true&_type=blogs&_r=4.

9. Kim Bhasin, "TOMS Shoe Founder to Critics: We Are Not 'Holier-Than-Thou,'"
Huff Post Small Business, *Huffington Post*, June 26, 2013, www.huffingtonpost.com
/2013/06/26/toms-shoes-criticism_n_3498840.html.

10. Bhasin, "TOMS Shoe Founder."

11. Herrera, "Questioning the TOMS Shoes Model."

12. Jacqueline Charles, "Haiti to Begin Manufacturing TOMS Shoes," *Miami Herald*, September 27, 2013, www.miamiherald.com/2013/09/27/3655205/haiti-to-begin-manufacturing-toms.html.

13. Morgan Clendaniel, "TOMS Glasses: The Newest Buy-One-Give-One Product from TOMS Shoes," *Fast Company*, June 7, 2011, www.fastcompany.com/1758060/toms-glasses -newest-buy-one-give-one-product-toms-shoes.

14. Scott Bessenecker, "Dismantling My American Messianic Complex," *The Least of These* (blog), InterVarsity, January 18, 2013, https://urbana.org/blogs/least-these/dismantling-my-american-messianic-complex.

15. Chimamanda Ngozi Adichie, "The Danger of a Single Story," TED, October 2009, transcript, www.ted.com/talks/chimamanda_adichie_the_danger_of_a_single_story/transcript.

16. Adichie, "The Danger."

17. "Haiti Quake Death Toll Rises to 230,000," BBC News, February 11, 2010, http://news.bbc.co.uk/2/hi/americas/8507531.stm.

18. "Red Cross: 3M Haitians Affected by Quake," CBS News, January 13, 2010, www.cbsnews.com/stories/2010/01/13/world/main6090601.shtml?tag=cbsnewsSectionContent.4.

19. Lee Ferran et al., "Haiti Rescue Efforts a Mix of Elation and Grief," ABC News, January 18, 2010, http://abcnews.go.com/GMA/HaitiEarthquake/earthquake-haiti-us-marines -aid-earthquake-relief-effort/story?id=9591220.

20. Mike Celizic, "U.S. Husband Pulls Wife from Haiti Rubble," *Today*, January 15, 2010, www.today.com/id/34841236/ns/today-today_news/t/us-husband-pulls-wife-haiti-rubble/.

21. Hal Bernton, "In Quake-Ravaged Haiti, Some Donations Miss the Mark," *Seattle Times*, March 23, 2010, http://seattletimes.com/html/localnews/2011421974_earthquakeaid24m.html.

22. Kathie Klarreich and Linda Polman, "The NGO Republic of Haiti," *The Nation*, November 19, 2012, www.thenation.com/article/170929/ngo-republic-haiti#.

23. Corbett and Fikkert, *When Helping Hurts*, 104–5.

24. "War in Darfur," *Wikipedia*, http://en.wikipedia.org/wiki/War_in_Darfur.

25. See Brian Fikkert, David Beckmann, and Dale Hanson Bourke, "Help That Makes a Difference: What's the Biggest Change Needed in How Charities and Federal Agencies Deliver Aid to Developing Nations?," *Christianity Today*, December 15, 2009, www.christianitytoday.com/ct/2009/december/14.54.html.

26. Fikkert, Beckmann, and Bourke, "Help That Makes a Difference."

27. See Corbett and Fikkert, *When Helping Hurts*, 151.

28. Jacqueline L. Salmon, "Churches Retool Mission Trips," *Washington Post*, July 5, 2008, http://articles.washingtonpost.com/2008-07-05/news/36816196_1_trips -christianity-today -free-health-clinic.

29. Shane Claiborne, *The Irresistible Revolution: Living as an Ordinary Radical* (Grand Rapids, MI: Zondervan, 2006), 295–96.

30. Casey McNerthney, "Man Found Dead in Ballard Park," Seattle 911—A Police and Crime Blog, *Seattle PI*, November 17, 2012, http://blog.seattlepi.com/seattle911 /2012/11/17/man-found-dead-in-ballard-park/.

Chapter 10—The Best Part of Wanting to Change the World

1. Gary A. Haugen, *Just Courage: God's Great Expedition for the Restless Christian* (Downers Grove, IL: InterVarsity Press, 2009), 125.

2. "Mother Teresa Quotes," Goodreads, http://www.goodreads.com/quotes/112196 -never-worry-about-numbers-help-one-person-at-a-time.

3. "Mother Teresa Quotes," Goodreads, http://www.goodreads.com/quotes/62266 -what-can-you-do-to-promote-world-peace-go-home.

4. Leroy Barber, *Everyday Missions: How Ordinary People Can Change the World* (Downers Grove, IL: InterVarsity Press, 2012), 17–18.

A portion of this book's proceeds will be donated to One Day's Wages—a movement of people, stories, and actions to fight extreme global poverty.

Join the movement. Learn how your day's wages, your ideas, or something as simple as your birthday can make a dramatic impact.

For more information, go to onedayswages.org.

You can follow Eugene on :

Twitter: @EugeneCho

Facebook: www.facebook.com/eugenecho

Instagram: http://instagram.com/seattlejediknight

Blog: EugeneCho.com